A Treatise on Advaita Vedānta

English Translation of

Vicāracandrodaya

of Pandit Pitambar

Contemporary Researches in Hindu Philosophy & Religion

(ISSN 0971-9628)

1. Idealistic Thought in Indian Philosophy; by Shuchita C. Divatia (ISBN 978-81-246-0021-4)
2. Karma and Reincarnation: The Vedāntic Perspective; by Muni Narayana Prasad (ISBN 978-81-246-0022-1)
3. Stonemill and Bhakti: From the Devotion of Peasant Women to the Philosophy of Swamies; by Guy Poitevin and Hema Rairkar (ISBN 978-81-246-0059-7)
4. Śaivism: Some Glimpses; by G.V. Tagare (ISBN 978-81-246-0076-4)
5. Advaita: A Conceptual Analysis; by A. Ramamurty (ISBN 978-81-246-0067-2)
6. Mind-Body Dualism: A Philosophic Investigation; by Alpana Chakraborty (ISBN 978-81-246-0071-9)
7. Hinduism and Scientific Quest; by T.R.R. Iyengar (ISBN 978-81-246-0077-1)
8. Indra and Other Vedic Deities — A Euhemeristic Study; by Uma Chakravarty (ISBN 978-81-246-0080-1)
9. Brahma-Vāda: Doctrine of Śrī Vallabhācārya; by G.V. Tagare (ISBN 978-81-246-0112-9)
10. The Science of Enlightenment: Enlightenment, Liberation and God — A Scientific Explanation; by Nitin Trasi (ISBN 978-81-246-0130-3)
11. Retrieving Sāṁkhya History: An Ascent from Dawn to Meridian; by Lallanji Gopal (ISBN 978-81-246-0143-3)
12. The Philosophical Foundations of Hinduism; by A. Ramamurty (ISBN 978-81-246-0163-1)
13. The Eternal Hinduism; by Baidyanath Saraswati (ISBN 978-81-246-0249-2)
14. Vedānta and its Philosophical Development; by A. Ramamurty (ISBN 978-81-246-0347-5)
15. Sāṁkhya-Yoga Epistomology; by Mukta Biswas (ISBN 978-81-246-0371-0)
16. A Sourcebook of Classical Hindu Thought; by Arvind Sharma (ISBN 978-81-246-0643-8)

Contemporary Researches in Hindu Philosophy & Religion, no. 17

A Treatise on Advaita Vedānta

English Translation of

Vicāracandrodaya

of Pandit Pitambar

by

S. Bhuvaneshwari

PRINTWORLD

Publishers of Indian Traditions

Cataloging in Publication Data — DK
[Courtesy: D.K. Agencies (P) Ltd. <docinfo@dkagencies.com>]

Pitambara, 1846 or 1847-
[Vicāracandrodaya. English]
A treatise on Advaita Vedānta : English translation of Vicāracandrodaya of Pandit Pitambar by S. Bhuvaneshwari.
p. cm. (Contemporary researches in Hindu philosophy & religion ; no. 17).
Includes verses in Hindi (Devanagari and roman).
Translated from Hindi.
Includes bibliographical references and index.
ISBN 9788124607077

1. Advaita. 2. Vedanta. I. Bhuvaneshwari, S., 1976- II. Title. III. Series : Contemporary researches in Hindu philosophy & religion ; no. 17.

DDC 181.482 23

ISBN 13: 978-81-246-0707-7 (HB)
ISBN 13: 978-81-246-0709-1 (PB)
First published in India in 2013

Printed and published by:
D.K. Printworld (P) Ltd.
Regd. Office : *'Vedaśrī'*, F-395, Sudarshan Park
(Metro Station: Ramesh Nagar)
New Delhi - 110 015
Phones : (011) 2545 3975; 2546 6019; *Fax* : (011) 2546 5926
e-mail : indology@dkprintworld.com
Web : www.dkprintworld.com

In remembrance of

J. Devanathan
(1982–2012)

a true friend
and
a committed philosopher

Pandit Pitambar (Vikram Saṁvat 1903-56)

Preface

VICĀRACANDRODAYA is a preliminary text (*prakaraṇa*) in Old Hindi (one of the regional mixed dialects) elucidating the basic concepts of Advaita Vedānta in the form of questions and answers. It is authored by Pandit Pitambar (Vikram Saṁvat 1903-56, CE 1846/47–1899/1900), the celebrated commentator (*ṭippaṇīkāra*) of the *magnum opus*, *Vicārasāgara*, an Advaitic work of Niścaladāsa Pitambar is eulogized as one of the preceptors in the tradition of Advaita Vedānta who has contributed immensely through his teachings and writings mainly in Hindi. Born in 1846/47CE in a small village "Anjar" in the city of Kutch (Gujarat), he was the second son of Pandit Purushottama and Viravati. He is said to have mastered Sanskrit and was engaged in the study of scriptures from a very early age. An account of his life is found in the introductory preface to *Vicāracandrodaya* in Hindi published by Khemraj Krishnadas, Bombay, in 2007.

A list of his works, both published and unpublished, is given in the introduction to the text *Vicārasāgara* of Niścaladāsa in Hindi published by Khemraj Krishnadas, Bombay, in 1994. Based on this, we get to know about some of the independent *prakaraṇas* written by Pitambar as *Bālabodha*, *Sarvātmabhāvapradīpa* and *Vedastuti*. Pitambar has also written a commentary titled *Vr̥ttiratnāvalī* for Niścaladāsa's *Vr̥ttiprabhākara* and a *ṭīkā* on the *Viparyaya* of Sundaravilāsa. He has contributed in the form of *ṭippaṇīs* to the works like *Pañcadaśī* and *Manoharmālā*. His rather only work in Sanskrit is *Śrutiṣaṭliṅgasaṁgrahaḥ* with his own brief commentary in Hindi. Some of his unpublished works mentioned are

Vedāntakośa (13 vols.), *Bodharatnākara*, *Pramādamudgara*, *Praśnottarakadamba*, *Ṣaṭdarśanasārāvalī*, *Mohajit Kathā*, *Sadācāradarpaṇa*, *Jñānagati* and *Saṁśayasudarśana*. His usual style is such that he writes generally a *ṭīkā* and *ṭippaṇī* for his own works. In *Vicāracandrodaya* too he clarifies various concepts and supplies further ideas in the form of *ṭippaṇī*s. The author refers to his own works in *ṭippaṇī*s 66 and 174 that are yet to be spotted.

The title *Vicāracandrodaya*, Pitambar explains (in his preface) as the rise of moon which dispels darkness. He states that a seeker who studies this text under a *brahmaniṣṭha guru*, will assimilate this teaching, in whose space-like mind will certainly rise knowledge compared to moon that beholds the youth state, in the form of enquiry, which will dispel darkness in the form of ignorance along with doubt and delusion. Pitambar concludes in his preface that this work should be studied from a *guru* with *śraddhā* and should not be studied independently since the "secret knowledge" of Vedānta is impossible to be grasped without the guidance of a *guru*. The significance of the title *Vicāracandrodaya* can also be interpreted as a complete work, in the sense, just as the full (*pūrṇa*) moon rises to dispel darkness on a full-moon day, likewise by an enquiry guided through these fifteen chapters one is "complete" in whom the ignorance-darkness is dispelled.

Pitambar presents his work in the form of a dialogue between the disciple and a *guru*, wherein 249 questions are taken up spread over fifteen chapters, with 179 *ṭippaṇī*s and he provides a concise lexicon of Vedānta in the sixteenth digit. This work is an essence of the entire Vedānta Śastra. Each chapter is named as *kalā* (digit). The digits begin by elucidating the essence of that particular chapter in poetry form. The poetic renderings of thirty-eight couplets in all these digits end with a declaration of Pitambar's conviction in Advaitic knowledge. The first chapter or digit introduces the subject matter of Vedānta, it highlights the importance of enquiry and enumerates the method of enquiry that is taken up in the following digits. The second digit introduces the method of superimposition and negation and in the following three digits — third, fourth and fifth — the application of this method is elaborated. The sixth digit deals with the culminating key concept of Advaita, i.e. proving the falsity of the world. After negation of the world, the nature of Self is discussed from digits seven to ten. In digit eleven, the knowledge of oneness is arrived through an enquiry into the *mahāvākya*. The consequence of self-knowledge is described in digits twelve, thirteen and fourteen. The nature of liberation and means to liberation are briefly mentioned in the fifteenth digit. The *Vedānta-padārtha-saṁjñā-varṇanam* dealing with various concepts of Vedānta ordered numerically is categorised as the sixteenth digit and this last chapter alone is not in the form of questions and answers but is presented more as an appendix. It is also known by the name *Laghu-vedānta-kośa*. The text concludes with a verse in Sanskrit.

An attempt to translate this work is a humble task to reach a large number of seekers for whom the regional language may be a barrier. Also, the objective here is to highlight the contribution of Pandit Pitambar to Advaita Vedānta, especially in the language (old Hindi) of the commoner. The translation is based on the edition published in the year 2007 (by Khemraj Krishnadas, Mumbai) and it is the ninth reprint. In the seventh reprint, the publisher mentions that Pitambar's Sanskrit work *Śrutiṣaṭliṅgasaṅgraha* with his own commentary in Hindi has been inserted as part A of the sixteenth chapter and the sixteenth chapter originally titled *Vedānta-padārtha-saṁjñā-varṇanam* is presented as part B of the sixteenth chapter. From then on, *Vicāracandrodaya* is published with sixteen chapters, with the sixteenth chapter containing two parts. However, in this translated work, the work of Pitambar is retained as published prior to the seventh reprint, i.e. containing sixteen chapters without the division of the sixteenth chapter into two parts, since that is the original work. An index at the end of the sixteenth chapter is provided for quick reference to the basic concepts of Advaita Vedānta. Occasionally, alternate words or phrases are provided within square brackets [ ] to help in understanding the translated portion. In the sixteenth chapter, certain concepts are just enumerated and not explained in the original work, in such cases, the translation or idea is again supplied within square brackets [ ].

This work can serve both as a guide to the beginners of Vedānta and also as a text for *nididhyāsana*. Here, not only the concepts are enumerated and defined but their philosophical application and significance are also pointed out as in sixth digit and *ṭippaṇī*s 119 to 130 and 149 that is beneficial for the beginners. The elaboration of the method of negation as found in Questions 49, 74, 129 and 172 is useful for *nididhyāsana*. Also, this work forms a ready reference to the basic concepts as discussed in *Pañcadaśī* of Vidyāraṇya and *Vicārasāgara* of Niścaladāsa.

I hope this work will be found useful by all those who are interested in Advaita Vedānta. I take this opportunity to express my indebtedness to my Vedānta *guru*, Svami Paramarthananda Sarasvati who is my inspirational guide and strength.

I thank Shri J. Antony Raj, Artist of Dakshinachitra Museum, Chennai, for the pencil sketch of Pandit Pitambar.

I wish to express my sincere thanks to Susheel K. Mittal, Director of D.K. Printworld for his interest and ready acceptance to publish this work.

with Nārāyaṇa smṛti

Chennai, 14 January 2013 **S. Bhuvaneshwari**

Contents

Kalā 1

Introduction[1]

मनहर छंद (*Manahara* Metre)[2]

पुरुषइच्छाविषय पुरुषार्थ जोई सोई।
दुःखनाश सुखप्राप्तिरूप मोक्ष मानहु।।

हेतु ताको ब्रह्मज्ञान सो परोक्ष अपरोक्ष।
तामैं अपरोक्ष दृढ अदृढ दो गानहु।।

मोक्षको साक्षात्हेतु दृढअपरोक्षज्ञान।
हेतु ता विचार जीवब्रह्मजग जानहु।।

तीनवस्तुरूप जड चेतनदो जड मिथ्या-
माया ब्रह्मचित् "सो मैं" पीतांबर स्यानहु।। १ ।।

puruṣa icchāviṣaya puruṣārtha joī soī ।
duḥkhanāśa sukhaprāptirūpa mokṣa mānahu ।।

hetu tāko brahmajñāna so parokṣa aparokṣa ।
tāmaiṅ aparokṣa dṛḍha adṛḍha do gānahu ।।

mokṣako sākṣāthetu dṛḍha aparokṣajñāna ।
hetu tā vicāra jīvabrahmajaga jānahu ।।

tīnavasturūpa jaḍa cetanado jaḍa mithyā-
māyā brahmacit "so maiṅ" pītāṁbara syānahu ।। 1 ।।

---

1 Introduction is that where other concepts are revealed keeping in mind the intended subject. It is like someone who desires to have a peep into another's house, with this intention, questions "does your cow give milk?", etc., by which other news is brought in which is called as introduction. Similarly, here, that which is intended to be taken up for enquiry is kept in mind based on which other terms like liberation are explicated is called Introduction.

2 This can be sung in any tune.

That which is desired by a human being is called human goal,
it is destruction of sorrow and attainment of peace, this is called liberation.

The means is knowledge of Brahman, which is indirect and direct,
of that direct is of two kinds, firm and uncertain.

The direct means to liberation is firm direct knowledge.
The means[3] is enquiry of *jīva*, *Brahman*, world, the nature of these three.

Inertness and Consciousness are two (of which) inert is false matter (*māyā*);
Brahman is Consciousness "is Me" Pitambar thus ascertains[4] ॥ 1 ॥

Q. 1: What is human goal (*puruṣārtha*)?

Ans: That which is the object of desire of all human beings is called human goal.[5]

Q. 2: What is the universal desire?

Ans: The entire humanity universally desires for the removal of sorrow and attainment of absolute happiness.

Q. 3: What do you mean by destroying sorrow and attaining absolute peace?

Ans: All sorrows[6] are removed[7] and absolute peace[8] is attained[9] — this is the nature of liberation.[10]

---

3 It is to be understood as "means" of firm direct knowledge.

4 This is to be ascertained in this manner.

5 *Dharma, artha, kāma* and *mokṣa,* these four are known as goal (*puruṣārtha*). Of these, the first three are secondary. Setting these aside, the last one is to be known as the primary human goal.

6 Sorrow is birth, death, etc., along with ignorance.

7 Removal is sublation in the form of conviction in falsity.

8 Absolute Peace is the content of highest love.

9 Like obtaining the "necklace [already] in the neck", it [liberation] is attainment of the eternally attained.

10 Remaining in the nature of oneself free from doership, →

Q. 4: How does one attain liberation?

Ans: Liberation is attained by *Brahman*-knowledge.[11]

Q. 5: What is *Brahman*-knowledge?[12]

Ans: *Brahman*-knowledge is cognition of the nature of *Brahman* as it is.

Q. 6: How many kinds of *Brahman*-knowledge are there?

Ans: *Brahman*-knowledge is of two kinds as indirect and direct.

Q. 7: What is indirect *Brahman*-knowledge?

Ans: (1. The nature of indirect *Brahman*-knowledge): The knowledge that *Brahman* is of the nature of Existence, Consciousness, Infinite is said to be indirect[13] *Brahman*-knowledge.

Q. 8: How is the indirect *Brahman*-knowledge attained?

Ans: (2. The means of indirect *Brahman*-knowledge): Faith in the words of *guru* and scriptures leads to indirect *Brahman*-knowledge.

Q. 9: What is the result of indirect *Brahman*-knowledge?

Ans: (3. The result of indirect *Brahman*-knowledge): By this the concealment in the form of veiling, resulting in non-existence (*asattva āpādaka-āvaraṇa*)[14] is destroyed.

→ enjoyership, etc., and other such limitations is liberation. Those who claim attainment of other worlds like *svarga, vaikuṇṭha, goloka* and *brahmaloka,* as liberation, they contradict the Vedas. The nature of liberation discussed above is based on the Vedas.

11 Action and meditation are the means for gaining refinement of mind and single-pointed concentration and they are not the [direct] means for attaining liberation.

12 Knowledge of *Brahman* as non-different from *ātmā*. It is the means for liberation.

13 The indirect knowledge indicates the meaning of the word "that" in the *mahāvākya* "that you are" [*tat tvam asi*] and it is beneficial in gaining the direct non-dual knowledge.

14 "*Brahman* does not exist", in this manner there is the result of →

Q. 10: When is indirect *Brahman*-knowledge said to be complete?

Ans: (4. The end of indirect *Brahman*-knowledge): The indirect *Brahman*-knowledge is complete when the nature of *Brahman* is ascertained as revealed by a *brahmaniṣṭha guru* and Vedānta scriptures.

Q. 11: What is direct *Brahman*-knowledge?

Ans: One who knows as "I am of the nature of Existence, Consciousness, Infinite *Brahman*" — it is called direct *Brahman*-knowledge.

Q. 12: How is direct *Brahman*-knowledge gained?

Ans: From a *guru* listening to the *mahāvākya tat tvam asi* etc., one gains the direct *Brahman*-knowledge.

Q. 13: How many kinds of direct *Brahman*-knowledge are there?

Ans: The direct *Brahman*-knowledge, as "uncertain" and "firm", is of two types.

Q. 14: What is uncertain direct *Brahman*-knowledge?

Ans: (1. Nature of uncertain direct *Brahman*-knowledge): Where the oneness of *Brahman* and *Ātman* is known along with (defects like) impossibility (*asambhāvanā*)[15] and contradictory notion (*viparīta bhāvanā*)[16] is called uncertain direct *Brahman*-knowledge.

→ the idea of non-existence which is concealment of Existent principle. This is called as concealment wherein the [knowledge of] non-existence is the result.

[15] (1) "Does Vedānta reveal the difference between *jīva* and *Brahman* or their oneness?" Such a doubt is related to the means of knowledge. And,

(2) "Is the difference between *jīva* and *Brahman* real or is the non-difference real?" Such a doubt is related to the object of knowledge. Both these kinds of doubt are known as impossibility (*asambhāvanā*).

[16] The difference between *jīva* and *Brahman* is real and the body, world, etc., are real, this is conviction in the contrary. It is called contradictory notion (*viparīta bhāvanā*).

Q. 15: What is the cause of uncertain direct *Brahman*-knowledge?

Ans: (2. The cause of uncertain direct *Brahman*-knowledge):

[1] The knowledge of varied scriptures with the defects of impurity (*mala*) and disturbance (*vikṣepa*).

[2] The notion of impossibility of non-duality of *Brahman*.

[3] The impressions caused by association with dualists and common people.

Along with (such defects) one who listens to the instruction of the *mahāvākya* from a *guru* it leads to uncertain direct *Brahman*-knowledge.

Q. 16: What is the result of uncertain direct *Brahman*-knowledge?

Ans: (3. The result of uncertain direct *Brahman*-knowledge): From uncertain direct *Brahman*-knowledge

[1] one attains higher worlds.

[2] one is born in pure, wealthy and respectable family or one is born in a family of enlightened ones as a result of their absence of [material] desire.

Q. 17: When is the uncertain direct *Brahman*-knowledge said to be complete?

Ans: (4. The end of uncertain direct *Brahman*-knowledge): Even when features of *Brahman* such as Existence, Consciousness and Infinite are directly known; then also doubt (*saṁśaya*)[17] and contradictory notion[18] persist; by this the uncertain direct *Brahman*-knowledge, is said to be complete.

Q. 18: What is the nature of firm direct *Brahman*-knowledge?

Ans: (1. Nature of firm direct *Brahman*-knowledge): That knowledge which is free from the two main defects, namely,

---

[17] [Unascertained] knowledge of two opposite views is known as doubt.

[18] Conviction in the contrary is said to be contradictory notion.

impossibility and contradictory notion, is firm direct *Brahman*-knowledge.

Q. 19: How is firm direct *Brahman*-knowledge attained?

Ans: (2. The cause of firm direct *Brahman*-knowledge): Listening to the meaning of the *mahāvākya*[19] directly from a *guru*, thereafter taking to an analysis in the form of *manana* and *nididhyāsana* leads to firm direct *Brahman*-knowledge.

Q. 20: What is the result of firm direct *Brahman*-knowledge?

Ans: (3. The result of firm direct *Brahman*-knowledge): The effects of ignorance being the non-illumination mode of concealment (*abhāna āpādaka-āvaraṇa*)[20] and modification (*vikṣepa*)[21] are eliminated along with ignorance and there is liberation in the form of attainment of *Brahman*.

Q. 21: When is the firm direct *Brahman*-knowledge complete?

Ans: (4. The completion of firm direct *Brahman*-knowledge): When the knowledge of "I" with regard to body is negated by the knowledge of *Brahman* as non-different from *ātmā* then the firm direct *Brahman*-knowledge is complete.

Q. 22: What is meant by enquiry?

Ans: (1. Nature of enquiry): Understanding the nature of self (*ātmā*) and non-self (*anātmā*) distinctly.

Q. 23: How does such an enquiry take place?

Ans: (2. Cause of enquiry): The enquiry takes place by the

---

19 The statement that reveals the oneness of *jīva* and *Brahman* is known as *mahāvākya*.

20 "*Brahman* does not shine" in this manner due to non-illumination [mode of concealment] there is non-apprehension of *Brahman* and it is the result of concealment known as *abhāna-āpādaka-āvaraṇa*.

21 The gross, subtle bodies along with reflected consciousness and the properties like doership, enjoyership, birth, death, etc., are known as *vikṣepa*.

grace of *Īśvara*, Veda, *guru* and one's own mind. By the grace of these four[22] the enquiry takes place.

Q. 24: What is the benefit of such an enquiry?

Ans: (3. The benefit of enquiry): By such an enquiry one attains firm direct *Brahman*-knowledge.

Q. 25: What marks the completion of this enquiry?

Ans: (4. The end of enquiry): The enquiry is complete when the firm direct *Brahman*-knowledge is complete.

Q. 26: What is to be enquired into?

Ans: (5. The content of enquiry):

[1] Who am I?

[2] What is *Brahman*?

[3] What is this world?

One should enquire into the nature of these three.

Q. 27: What is the general nature of these three entities?

Ans: [1-2] "I and *Brahman*" are Consciousness and [3] — the world[23] is matter.

Q. 28: What is Consciousness?

Ans: 1. It is of the nature of Knowledge.

2. It knows the entire inert world like pot etc. and

3. which cannot be known by mind, sense-organ, etc. This is Consciousness.

---

22 (1) Attainment of *sadguru* etc., and factors facilitating knowledge is the grace of *Īśvara*.

(2) The power to retain [in memory] the meaning of the scriptures is the grace of Veda.

(3) The valid teaching based on scriptures and one's own life-experience is the grace of *guru*.

(4) Following the means as instructed by the scriptures and *guru* is the grace of one's own mind.

23 World is the macro and micro gross, subtle and causal bodies with respective states and properties.

Q. 29: What is Matter?

Ans: 1. That which does not know itself

2. nor does it know others is called matter.

Matter is Ignorance[24] that includes its products made of elements[25] and elementals.[26] This is inert entity.

Q. 30: What is the benefit of such an enquiry of the three entities as mentioned above?

Ans: (6. The Benefit of Enquiry):

[1] The words *tat* and *tvam* in the *mahāvākya tat tvam asi* in their primary meaning refer to *jīva*[27] and *Īśvara*[28] with the world[29] as adjunct. Just as the error of "snake" in rope, "human" in tree trunk and mirage-water in desert are dismissed as false on scrutiny, so also an enquiry into the nature of the world is beneficial.

[2] "I am (secondary meaning of the word *tvam*) *Brahman* (secondary meaning of the word *tat*)", in this way the oneness of *Brahman* and *Ātmā* on enquiry leads to reality. This is the benefit of enquiry into "who am I" and "what is *Brahman*".

Q. 31: Who is eligible for such an enquiry and what should such a one do?

---

24 "I don't know" the cause of such an expression is ignorance which is beginningless with the powers of concealment and projection.

25 The five elements, namely space, earth, etc.

26 The products of the elements, namely the macro and the micro, are the elementals.

27 *Jīva* is *kūṭastha* — consciousness with internal organ and reflected consciousness.

28 *Īśvara* is *Brahman* — Consciousness with *māyā* and reflected consciousness.

29 The three bodies at the macro and micro levels, the five sheaths, the three states of experience, etc., name and form are known as the world.

Ans: (7. Qualification for enquiry):

[1] The eligible person (*adhikārī*) for this enquiry is an intense seeker (*uttama jijñāsu*).[30]

[2] That *adhikārī* by the grace of *sadguru* takes to enquiry of the Introduction and other aspects (*prakriyās*)[31] [of *Vicāracandrodaya*] and attains the direct knowledge "I am *Brahman*".

Q. 32: What is the name of the *prakriyās*?

1. Introduction
2. Superimposition and negation of the world
3. I am the witness of the three bodies
4. I am beyond the five sheaths
5. I am the witness of the three states
6. Falsity of the world
7. "Features" of Self
8. Existence, Consciousness, Absolute Peace [Infinite]
9. Indescribability
10. General and Specific Consciousnesses
11. Establishment of oneness of the word-meanings of *tat* and *tvam*
12. Destruction of *karma* in the Enlightened
13. The seven *jñāna-bhūmikās*
14. *Jīvanmukti* and *Videhamukti*

---

30 One who has the fourfold qualities of discrimination, dispassion, sixfold-mental disciplines and desire for liberation with faith in the words of *brahmavit guru* and scriptures, without taking to dry logic (*kutarka*), such a one with an intense desire [to gain knowledge] is the *adhikārī* who is said to be *uttama jijñāsu*.

31 Any [particular] method of understanding Advaita is known as *prakriyā*.

15. The object of Vedānta

These are the names of the *prakriyās*.[32]

Thus ends the first digit of *Vicāracandrodaya* titled "Introduction"

---

[32] (1) Analysis of the world is done in the *prakriyā* of Digits 1, 2, 6, 12 and 13 [of *Vicāracandrodaya*].

(2) "Who am I along with the world?" This is analysed in *prakriyās* of Digits 3-5.

(3) Who is *Paramātmā*? This analysis occurs in the *prakriyā* of Digit 10.

(4) The nature of *Brahman* and *ātman* is found in the *prakriyā* of Digits 7-9, 11 and 14.

(5) The nature of world and *Brahman-ātman* is done in the *prakriyā* of Digit 15.

All these *prakriyās* are helpful in the analysis of the word-meaning of *tat* and *tvam* and in the conviction of oneness. [Digit 16 is not a *prakriyā* but enumeration of Advaitic concepts in a nutshell.]

Kalā 2

Superimposition and Negation of the World

मनहर छंद (*Manahara* Metre)

प्रपंचारोपापवाद करि निष्प्रपंच वस्तु।
ब्रह्मजानिके अवस्तु – मायादिक भानिये।।

ब्रह्म माया संबंध रु जीवईश भेद तिन।
षट् ये अनादि तामैं ब्रह्मानंत मानिये।।

वस्तुमैं अवस्तु कर कथन आरोप बाधि-
अवस्तु वस्तुकथन अपवाद गानिये।।

गुरुके प्रसाद यह युक्ति जानि पीतांबर।
तज तमका रज आरज निज जानिये।। २ ।।

prapañcāropāpavāda kari niṣprapañca vastu ।
brahmajānike avastu — māyādika bhāniye ।।

brahma māyā sambandha ru jīvaīśa bheda tina ।
ṣaṭ ye anādi tāmaiṁ brahmānaṅta māniye ।।

vastumaiṁ avastu kara kathana āropa bādhi-
avastu vastukathana apavāda gāniye ।।

guruke prasāda yaha yukti jāni pītāṁbara ।
taja tamakā raja āraja nija jāniye ।। 2 ।।

In superimposition and negation of world, the entity devoid of world
is *Brahman; māyā* etc. are non-entities.

Brahman, māyā, their relation, *jīva, Īśvara*, their difference — these six are without a beginning of which *Brahman* is endless [limitless].

Superimposition is seeing in an entity another entity. The sublated[33]
non-entity in a thing is to be known as negation.

Pitambar received this reasoning by the grace of the *guru*,
O Seeker! May you know the nature of yourself[34] ||2||

Q. 33: How does the superimposition[35] of world on Pure Consciousness happen?

Ans: Upon the beginningless Pure Consciousness there is the beginningless[36] imagined (*kalpita*)[37] matter (*prakṛti*). This *prakṛti* has a beginningless superimposed relationship of identity with *Brahman*. That is, along with the superimposition of difference there is a real relation of non-difference. That *prakṛti* is also known as (1) *māyā*, (2) *avidyā*, and (3) *tamas*.

Pradhāna or *prakṛti* is known in these divisions, i.e.

1. that which is of pure *sattva guṇa*[38] is called *māyā*,
2. that which is of impure *sattva guṇa*[39] is called *avidyā*, and

---

33 Prose-reading: Negation of non-entity and the [essential] substance as the remainder is sublation.

34 Prose-reading: O Seeker, who is a discriminative one. May you know (the essential nature of) yourself.

35 *Brahman* is the entity on which, ignorance and its effects that are non-entities, are seen, is known as superimposition.

36 An entity without origination is by nature without a beginning. In this way is pure *Brahman*, *prakṛti*, their relation, *Īśvara*, *jīva* and their difference. These are six and by the principle of continuity (*pravāha*) the world is also said to be without a beginning.

37 That which has not happened and is a delusion like the dream objects is known as imagined (*kalpita*).

38 Just as a brāhmaṇa king cannot be suppressed by a kṣatriya and śūdra ministers, that is, *sattva* subdues *rajas* and *tamas*. It is pure *sattva guṇa*.

39 Just as two śūdra princes overpower a brāhmaṇa minister, here the *rajas* and *tamas* subdue *sattva*. It is impure *sattva guṇa*.

3. that which consists of *tamoguṇa* is matter predominant with the nature of *tamas*.

1. In *māyā* is the reflection of *Brahman*. That substratum (*Brahman*) along with *māyā*[40] is the creator of the world who is the omniscient *Īśvara*.

2. In *avidyā* is the reflection of *Brahman*. That substratum (*kūṭastha*) along with *avidyā* is the experiencer *jīva* with limited knowledge.

1. That *Īśvara* and *jīva* are beginningless. The limiting adjunct of *Īśvara* is *māyā* which is one and is of the nature of relative pervasiveness (*āpekṣika-vyāpaka*).[41] Hence *Īśvara* is also one and all-pervasive.

2. The limiting adjunct of *jīva* is the manifold *avidyā* which is limited. Hence *jīva* is also many and limited.

The difference between *jīva* and *Īśvara* is a beginningless superimposition.

1. Before creation, *avidyā* which is the limiting factor of *jīva* is resolved in *māyā* along with the *karma* of the *jīvas*. That *māyā* like the *avidyā* in deep sleep state is non-different from *Brahman*. Thus, prior to creation, there was one, non-dual existent, consciousness, infinite *Brahman* without homogeneous, heterogeneous and internal divisions.

2. *Brahman* at the beginning of creation, on ripening of the

---

40 The word *māyā* here means *māyā* itself and the word *tamas* refers to *pradhāna prakṛti*. These two serve as the adjuncts:

1. With the adjunct of *māyā*, *Īśvara*, like a potter, is the intelligent cause of the universe.

2. With the adjunct *tamas*, *pradhāna prakṛti*, *Īśvara*, like the clay, is the material cause of the universe.

41 From a standpoint, that which is said to be pervasive or limited is referred to as of the nature of relative pervasiveness. Like a house which is pervasive from the standpoint of pot etc., but is limited from the standpoint of a village is said to be of the →

karma of the *jīvas*, expresses the desire that "I am one, let me multiply".

3. Due to such a desire, a disturbance is caused in *māyā*, the adjunct of *Brahman* and, in order, the five elements — space, air, fire, water and earth emerge.
4. They do not undergo the process of grossification (*pañcīkaraṇa*). They are non-grossified. From these emerge the macro and micro subtle creations. Then by the desire of *Īśvara* they undergo the process of grossification. From the grossified five elements emerge the macro and micro gross creation.
5. From the standpoint of *jīva*, one who identifies with the macro gross, subtle and causal universe is *Īśvara*, and *jīva* is one who identifies with the micro gross, subtle and causal non-world [body]. Of which, *Īśvara* being omniscient is ever-liberated and *jīva* with limited knowledge is bound.

In this manner, the world is superimposed on Pure Consciousness.

Q. 34: Is such a superimposition real or unreal?

Ans: This superimposition is false like the "snake" in rope, "dream" in the witness consciousness and reflection of a city in a mirror.

Q. 35: What causes such a superimposition?

Ans: Such a superimposition happens because of ignorance.

Q. 36: When does such a superimposition take place and why does it happen? How should one analyse this?

Ans: It is like an oil stain on a person's cloth. When the person sees the stain he engages in removing the stain and does not

→ nature of relative pervasiveness. Similarly, *māyā* also is pervasive from the standpoint of earth etc. and from the standpoint of *Brahman* it is limited which is referred to as relative pervasiveness.

involve into an enquiry of "how the cloth got stained?" since such an enquiry is purposeless [now]. There is no use in engaging in questions like when was this world superimposed and why?" but it is worth getting into the solutions for removal of such an error.

Q. 37: What is the method of removal of such a superimposition?

Ans: By the knowledge of *Brahman*

1. *māyā* and *avidyā* are removed.
2. the *prakṛti* along with its effects are removed.
3. the relation between *prakṛti* and *Brahman* is removed.
4. the notion of *jīva* and *Īśvara* is removed.
5. the difference between *jīva* and *Īśvara* is removed.
6. the bondage is removed and liberation is attained.

In this way, the superimposition is removed at one sweep which is known as negation.[42]

Q. 38: How does the knowledge of *Brahman* occur?

Ans: The knowledge of *Brahman* is gained by an enquiry as analysed in the following sections.

Thus ends the second digit of *Vicāracandrodaya* titled "Superimposition and Negation of the World"

42 Just as the rope remains on negation of "snake" and its knowledge; similarly on negation of the world and its knowledge what remains is pure *Brahman*, the substratum.

Kalā 3

I Am the Witness of the Three Bodies

मनहर छंद (*Manahara* Metre)

द्रष्टा तीनदेहको मैं स्थूल सूक्ष्म कारण ये।
तीनदेह दृश्य अरु अनातमा मानियो।।

पंचीकृतपंचभूतके पचीसतत्त्वनको।
स्थूलदेह एह भोगआयतन गानियो।।

अपंचीकृतभूतके सरुदशतत्त्वनको।
सूक्ष्मदेह होई भोगसाधन प्रमानियो।।

अज्ञान कारणदेह घटवत दृश्य एह।
पीतांबर द्रष्टा आप जानि दृश्य भानियो।। ३ ।।

draṣṭā tīnadehako maiṁ sthūla sūkṣma kāraṇa ye ।
tīnadeha dr̥śya aru anātamā māniyo ।।

pañcīkr̥tapañcabhūtake pacīsatattvanako ।
sthūladeha eha bhoga āyatana gāniyo ।।

apañcīkr̥tabhūtake saptadaśatattvanako ।
sūkṣmadeha hoī bhogasādhana pramāniyo ।।

ajñāna kāraṇadeha ghaṭavata dr̥śya eha ।
pītāṁbara draṣṭā āpa jāni dr̥śya bhāniyo ।। 3 ।।

I am the "seer" of the three bodies — gross, subtle and causal.
These three bodies are seen and are to be known as non-self.

The grossified five elements, with twenty-five principles,
are the gross body which is the abode of experience.

The non-grossified elements with seventeen entities
is the subtle body which is the means of experience.

The ignorance causal body like a pot is seen
Pitambar is the "seer" different from the seen. ॥3॥

Q. 39: The first *prakriyā* is — "I am the witness of the three bodies". What are the three bodies?

Ans: The gross, subtle and causal are the three bodies.

1. I Am the Witness of the Gross Body

Q. 40: What is gross body?

Ans: The grossified five great elements with twenty-five principles together are known as the gross body.

Q. 41: What are the five great elements?

Ans: Space, air, fire, water and earth are the five great elements.

Q. 42: What are the twenty-five principles of the five great elements?

Ans: (1-5) The five principles of space: desire,[43] anger, sorrow, delusion[44] and fear.

(6-10) The five principles of air: moving, circling, running, expanding and contracting.

(7-15) The five principles of fire: hunger, thirst, laziness, sleep and splendour.

(16-20) The five principles of water: sperm (*śukra*) or power (*vīrya*), egg or blood, spit, urine and sweat.

(21-25) The five principles of earth: bone, flesh, pulse (*nāḍī*), skin and hair.

These are the twenty-five aspects of the five great elements.

Q. 43: What is meant by grossified five great elements?

---

[43] Yearning for any kind of experience is known as desire.

[44] The notion of "I-ness" and "mine-ness" is known as delusion.

Ans: The five elements that undergo the process of grossification[45] is said to be grossified five great elements.

Q. 44: What is grossification?

Ans: Each of the five elements split into two equal halves and now there are ten parts. Of which the first five parts remain [undivided] and the other five parts divide further into four equal parts. Each of the four parts is shared with the other elements and one part remains with each element. Thus, one part remains as it is and the other part into four are shared. This process is known as grossification.

Q. 45: In what manner the five elements mutually combine?

Ans: Example: Like five friends gather mango, banana, etc. and consume together. Where each of them cut the fruit into two, keep one half with them and divide the other half into four and share the four parts with each other. Then there is the mixture of fruits among the five friends.

Application of the example:

[1] Space splits into two halves, of which

1. one half remains and
2. the second half divides itself into four parts.

   These do not mix with space and

   [1] one mixes with air,

   [2] one mixes with fire,

   [3] one mixes with water, and

   [4] one mixes with earth.

[2] Air splits into two halves, of which

1. one half remains and

---

45 First, there were the non-grossified five elements. Then by the desire of *Īśvara* the process of grossification happened resulting in the gross universe for the experience of the *jīvas*.

2. the second half divides itself into four parts. These do not mix with air and
   [1] one mixes with space,
   [2] one mixes with fire,
   [3] one mixes with water, and
   [4] one mixes with earth.

[3] Fire splits into two halves, of which
1. one half remains and
2. the second half divides itself into four parts. These do not mix with fire and
   [1] one mixes with space,
   [2] one mixes with air,
   [3] one mixes with water, and
   [4] one mixes with earth.

[4] Water splits into two halves, of which
1. one half remains and
2. the second half divides itself into four parts. These do not mix with water and
   [1] one mixes with space,
   [2] one mixes with air,
   [3] one mixes with fire, and
   [4] one mixes with earth.

[5] Earth splits into two halves, of which
1. one half remains and
2. the second half divides itself into four parts. These do not mix with earth and
   [1] one mixes with space,
   [2] one mixes with air,

[3] one mixes with fire, and

[4] one mixes with water.

In this way, there are twenty-five principles as the result of the mutual mixture of the five great elements.

Q. 46: How does the twenty-five principles of the five great elements occur?

Ans: Each element has its own primary half and secondary parts of the other elements. By this, each element produces five different principles and thus altogether there are twenty-five principles.

Q. 47: What are the twenty-five principles pertaining to the gross body?

Ans: [1-5] The five principles of space:[46] (1) sorrow, (2) desire, (3) anger, (4) delusion, and (5) fear. Of these,

1. Sorrow[47] is the primary part of space. It is said that when

---

[46] Some text considers the five *tattva*s of the space element as the space in the regions like the head, neck, heart, belly and hip.

(1) The space in the head region is the primary part of space element and it is the substratum of the *anāhata* sound.

(2) The space in the neck region is that of air. It is the abode of inhalation and exhalation.

(3) The space in the heart is that of fire. It is the abode of *pitta*.

(4) The space within the belly is the part of water. It is the abode of the consumed water.

(5) The space occupied by the hip region is the part of earth. It is the base of sense of smell.

In this description, desire, anger, etc. cannot be the principles of the gross body. But they are the characteristics of the subtle body. Other texts consider desire, etc. as the primary feature of the subtle body. The gross body is like a pot that is cool because of cold water in it; similarly, the features of subtle body are felt in the gross body and hence they are known as the secondary features of the gross body.

[47] Even though in the division of elements like air etc., there is a

→

there arises sorrow then the body is felt vacuum and the space is also vacuum. Hence, it [sorrow] is the primary part of space.

2. Desire[48] — in space there is mixture of part of air. It is said that the mental modifications in the form of desires is unstable and air is also unstable. Hence it [desire] is said as the part of air.
3. Anger — in space there is mixture of part of fire. It is said when anger arises then the body gets heated up and the fire is also of the nature of heat. So, it [anger] is the part of fire.
4. Delusion — in space there is mixture of part of water. It is said that there is extension of delusion towards son etc. and the drops of water also extend or spread. Hence it [delusion] is part of water.
5. Fear — in space there is mixture of part of earth. It is said that when there is fear the body becomes inert and motionless and the earth also is inert in nature and hence it [fear] is part of earth.

[6-10] The five principles of air: (6) expanding, (7) running, (8) turning, (9) moving, and (10) contracting.

6. Expanding — in air there is the mixture of part of space. The principle of expansion is found in space and hence it [expanding] is part of space.
7. Running — it is the primary part of air. It is said that the principle of running is found in air and hence it [running] is the primary part of air.

→ mixture of one part of space and therefore there is no primary part of space element alone, then also, sorrow and space share a commonness. Hence, sorrow is the primary part of space. Some say, greed is like space, which leaves emptiness even after attainment of objects and hence it is the primary part of space. Other elements also are to be understood in this manner.

48 As son is like father, desire is like air. It is part of air. In the same way, other elements are to be understood.

8. Turning — in air there is the mixture of part of fire. The turning pertains to the limbs and the brightness of fire also turns or circulates. So, it [turning] is part of fire.
9. Moving — the air consists of mixture of part of water. It is said that movement refers to moving and water also moves. Hence it [moving] is part of water.
10. Contracting — in air there is the mixture of part of earth. It is said that contraction is withering in and in earth this contraction is found. So, it [contracting] is part of earth.

[11-15] The five principles of fire are: (11) sleep, (12) thirst, (13) hunger, (15) brilliance, and (16) laziness.

11. Sleep — in fire there is the mixture of part of space. It is said that when sleep occurs the body is felt empty and the space is also vacuum. So, it [sleep] is part of space.
12. Thirst — in fire there is the mixture of part of air. It is said that thirst dries up the throat and air also dries up wet clothes, etc. Hence it [thirst] is part of air.
13. Hunger — it is the primary part of fire. It is said that in hunger whatever is consumed is burnt down and similarly whatever comes in contact with fire is reduced to ashes. So, it [hunger] is part of fire.
14. Brilliance — in fire there is mixture of part of water. It is said that due to heat there is brilliance and likewise water also is formed due to heat. So, it [brilliance] is part of water.
15. Laziness — in fire there is mixture of part of earth. It is said that due to laziness the body is felt as inert and earth is also inert in nature. So, it [laziness] is part of earth.

[16-20] The five principles of water are: (16) saliva, (17) perspiration, (18) urine, (19) sperm, and (20) egg.

16. Saliva — in water there is mixture of part of space. It is said that the saliva varies as high and low, and there is also high and low of space. Hence, it [saliva] is part of space.

17. Perspiration — in water there is mixture of part of air. It is said that perspiration is an outcome of hard work and air also is produced with effort by fanning, etc. So, it [perspiration] is part of air.

18. Urine — in water there is the mixture of part of fire. It is said to be hot and fire is also hot. So it [urine] is part of fire.

19. Sperm — it is the primary part of water. It is said that sperm is white in colour and is the cause for conception likewise water is also white in colour and is the cause for tree [growth of tree]. So, it [sperm] is part of water.

20. Egg — in water there is the mixture of part of earth. It is said that egg is red in colour and earth is also red in colour. So, it [egg] is part of earth.

[21-25] The five principles of earth are: (21) hair, (22) skin, (23) pulse, (24) flesh, and (25) bone.

21. Hair[49] — in earth there is the mixture of part of space. It is said that hair is empty. One does not experience pain when it is cut. Similarly, space is also empty. So, it [hair] is part of space.

22. Skin — in earth there is the mixture of part of air. It is said that skin senses touch of cold, heat, hard, soft and air also possesses the quality of touch. So it [skin] is part of air.

23. Pulse — in earth there is the mixture of part of fire. It is said that the temperature is examined through the pulse and fire is also of the form of heat. Hence it [pulse] is part of fire.

---

49 [It refers to] the hair on the head. It includes hair in other parts of the body.

24. Flesh — in earth there is the mixture of part of water. It is said that flesh is wet and water is also wet. So, it [flesh] is part of water.

25. Bone[50] — it is the primary part of earth. It is said that it (bone) is hard and yellow in colour. Earth is also hard and is of yellow colour. So, it [bone] is primary part of earth.

In this manner, there are twenty-five principles in the gross body.

Q. 48: What is the purpose of knowing these twenty-five principles?

Ans: [1] I am not these twenty-five principles and

[2] these twenty-five principle are not mine.

[3] These twenty-five principles belong to the grossified five great elements.

[4] I, who know these twenty-five principles, like the seer of a pot, am different from them.

It is to be ascertained in this manner. This is the benefit of knowing these twenty-five principles.

Q. 49: How should one know that "I am not these twenty-five principles and they are not mine"?

Ans: (1-5) The five aspects of space:

(1) [1] When there is sorrow, I know and

[2] when there is no sorrow, I know its absence also.

Therefore,

[1] I am not this sorrow.

[2] This sorrow is not mine.

[3] This sorrow belongs to space.

[4] I, the knower of sorrow, like the knower of pot, am different from it.

50 Nail and teeth are included in [the categorization of] bone.

Thus, sorrow is not me and it is not mine. This is to be known.

(2) [1] When there is desire, I know.

[2] When there is no desire, also I know its absence.[51]

Therefore,

[1] I am not this desire.

[2] This desire is not mine.

[3] This desire belongs to space.

[4] I, the knower of desire, like the knower of pot, am different from it.

Thus, desire is not me and it is not mine. This is to be known.

(3) [1] When there is anger, I know.

[2] When there is no anger, I know its absence also.

Therefore,

[1] I am not this anger.

[2] This anger is not mine.

[3] This anger belongs to space.

[4] I, the knower of anger, like the knower of pot, am different from it.

Thus, anger is not me and it is not mine. This is to be known.

(4) [1] When there is delusion, I know.

[2] When there is no delusion, I know its absence also.

---

[51] (1) The absence before the production of an effect is known as prior non-existence.

(2) The absence after the destruction [of effect] is known as posterior non-existence.

(3) The absence in three periods of time is known as absolute non-existence.

(4) The absence of an entity in another entity is known as mutual non-existence.

In this way, non-existence is of four kinds.

Therefore,

[1] I am not this delusion.

[2] This delusion is not mine.

[3] This delusion belongs to space.

[4] I, the knower of delusion, like the knower of pot, am different from it.

Thus, delusion is not me and it is not mine. This is to be known.

(5) [1] When there is fear, I know.

[2] When there is no fear, I know its absence also.

Therefore,

[1] I am not this fear.

[2] This fear is not mine.

[3] This fear belongs to space.

[4] I, the knower of fear, like the knower of pot, am different from it.

Thus, fear is not me and it is not mine. This is to be known.

(6-10) The five aspects of air:

(6) [1] When the body expands, I know.

[2] When the body does not expand, I know its absence also.

Therefore,

[1] I am not this expansion.

[2] This expansion is not mine.

[3] This expansion belongs to air.

[4] I, the knower of this expansion like the knower of pot, am different from it.

Such an expansion is not me and not mine. This should be known.

(7) [1] When the body runs [moves], I know.

[2] When the body does not run [move], I know its absence also.

Therefore,

[1] I am not this running [moving].

[2] This running [movement] is not mine.

[3] This running [movement] belongs to air.

[4] I, the knower of this running [movement] like the knower of pot, am different from it.

Such a running [movement] is not me and not mine. This should be known.

(8) [1] When the body turns around, I know.

[2] When the body does not turn around, I know its absence also.

Therefore,

[1] I am not this circulatory motion.

[2] This circulatory motion is not mine.

[3] This circulatory motion belongs to air.

[4] I, the knower of this circulatory motion like the knower of pot, am different from it.

Such a circulatory motion is not me and not mine. This should be known.

(9) [1] When the body moves, I know.

[2] When the body does not move, I know its absence also.

Therefore,

[1] I am not this locomotion.

[2] This locomotion is not mine.

[3] This locomotion belongs to air.

[4] I, the knower of this locomotion like the knower of pot, am different from it.

Such a locomotion is not me and not mine. This should be known.

(10) [1] When the body contracts, I know.

[2] When the body does not contract, I know its absence also.

Therefore,

[1] I am not this contraction.

[2] This contraction is not mine.

[3] This contraction belongs to air.

[4] I, the knower of this contraction like the knower of pot, am different from it.

Such a contraction is not me and not mine. This should be known.

(11-15) The five aspects of fire:

(11) [1] When there is sleep, I know.

[2] When there is no sleep, I know its absence also.

Therefore,

[1] I am not this sleep.

[2] This sleep is not mine.

[3] This sleep belongs to fire.

[4] I, the knower of this sleep like the knower of pot, am different from it.

Such a sleep is not me and not mine. This should be known.

(12) [1] When there is thirst, I know.

[2] When there is no thirst, I know its absence also.

Therefore,

[1] I am not this thirst.

[2] This thirst is not mine.

[3] This thirst belongs to fire.

[4] I, the knower of this thirst like the knower of pot, am different from it.

Such a thirst is not me and not mine. This should be known.

(13) [1] When there is hunger, I know.

[2] When is no hunger, I know its absence also.

Therefore,

[1] I am not this hunger.

[2] This hunger is not mine.

[3] This hunger belongs to fire.

[4] I, the knower of this hunger like the knower of pot, am different from it.

Such a hunger is not me and not mine. This should be known.

(14) [1] When there is brilliance, I know.

[2] When there is no brilliance, I know its absence also.

Therefore,

[1] I am not this brilliance.

[2] This brilliance is not mine.

[3] This brilliance belongs to fire.

[4] I, the knower of this brilliance like the knower of pot, am different from it.

Such a brilliance is not me and not mine. This should be known.

(15) [1] When there is lethargy, I know.

[2] When there is no lethargy, I know its absence also.

Therefore,

[1] I am not this lethargy.

[2] This lethargy is not mine.

[3] This lethargy belongs to fire.

[4] I, the knower of this lethargy like the knower of pot, am different from it.

Such a lethargy is not me and not mine. This should be known.

(16-20) The five aspects of water:

(16) [1] When there is saliva, I know.

[2] When there is no saliva, I know its absence also.

Therefore,

[1] I am not this saliva.

[2] This saliva is not mine.

[3] This saliva belongs to water.

[4] I, the knower of this saliva like the knower of pot, am different from it.

Such a saliva is not me and not mine. This should be known.

(17) [1] When there is perspiration, I know.

[2] When there is no perspiration, I know its absence also.

Therefore,

[1] I am not this perspiration.

[2] This perspiration is not mine.

[3] This perspiration belongs to water.

[4] I, the knower of this perspiration like the knower of pot, am different from it.

Such a perspiration is not me and not mine. This should be known.

(18) [1] When there is urine, I know.

[2] When there is no urine, I know its absence also.

Therefore,

[1] I am not this urine.

[2] This urine is not mine.

[3] This urine belongs to water.

[4] I, the knower of this urine like the knower of pot, am different from it.

Such a urine is not me and not mine. This should be known.

(19) [1] When there is semen that increases the virility in the body, I know.

[2] When there is no virility, I know its absence also.

Therefore,

[1] I am not this virility.

[2] This virility is not mine.

[3] This virility belongs to water.

[4] I, the knower of this virility like the knower of pot, am different from it.

Such virility is not me and not mine. This should be known.

(20) [1] When the blood increases in the body, I know.

[2] When there is no blood, I know its absence also.

Therefore,

[1] I am not this blood.

[2] This blood is not mine.

[3] This blood belongs to water.

[4] I, the knower of this blood like the knower of pot, am different from it.

Such a blood is not me and not mine. This should be known.

(21-25) The five aspects of earth:

(21) [1] When the hair grows, I know.

[2] When there is less hair, I know this decrease also.

Therefore,

[1] I am not this hair.

[2] This hair is not mine.

[3] This hair belongs to earth.

[4] I, the knower of this hair like the knower of pot, am different from it.

Such a hair is not me and not mine. This should be known.

(22) [1] When the sense-organ of skin grasps sense of touch, I know.

[2] When the skin does not grasp touch, I know its absence also.

Therefore,

[1] I am not the skin.

[2] This skin is not mine.

[3] This skin belongs to earth.

[4] I, the knower of this skin like the knower of pot, am different from it.

Such a skin is not me and not mine. This should be known.

(23) [1] When the pulse ticks, I know.

[2] When the pulse does not tick, I know its absence also.

Therefore,

[1] I am not the pulse.

[2] This pulse is not mine.

[3] This pulse belongs to earth.

[4] I, the knower of this pulse like the knower of pot, am different from it.

Such a pulse is not me and not mine. This should be known.

(24) [1] When the flesh grows, I know.

[2] When there is no flesh, I know its absence also.

Therefore,

[1] I am not the flesh.

[2] This flesh is not mine.

[3] This flesh belongs to earth.

[4] I, the knower of this flesh like the knower of pot, am different from it.

Such a flesh is not me and not mine. This should be known.

(25) [1] When the bone is unaffected, I know.

[2] When the bone is not unaffected, its absence also I know.

Therefore,

[1] I am not the bone.

[2] This bone is not mine.

[3] This bone belongs to earth.

[4] I, the knower of this bone like the knower of pot, am different from it.

Such a bone is not me and not mine. This should be known.

In this manner, that the twenty-five aspects are not me and not mine, is to be known.

Q. 50: "These twenty-five aspects are not me" by knowing this, what is certainly gained?

Ans: The gross body and its attributes — (1) name, (2) genus (*jāti*), (3) stage of life (*āśrama*), (4) class (*varṇa*), (5) relation, (6) modification, (7) birth and death, etc., are not me and not mine. Such a conviction arises.

Q. 51: How does one understand that "I am not the name and the name is not mine"?

Ans: 1. Name was not there before the birth.

2. Name is imagined after birth.

3. When each part of the body is investigated, name is not obtained.

Therefore,

1. I am not this name.
2. This name is not mine.
3. This name is imagined from the standpoint of the gross body.

4. I, the knower of the name like the knower of pot, am different from it.

Such a name is not me and not mine. This should be known.

Q. 52: How does one understand that I am not the *jāti* or *varṇa*?

Ans: 1. The class like brāhmaṇa etc., is an attribute of the gross body. It is not the quality of subtle body or of the Self. It is said that the subtle body and Self, which was the content of the past gross body, is the content of the present body and will be the content of the future body. The *jāti* of the previous body need not be the same for the present body and of the future body. Thus, the *jāti* as a quality belongs to the gross body. It is not the quality of the subtle body or Self.

2. On analysis of the limbs of the body, the *jāti* does not refer to the gross body also.

Therefore,

1. I am not the *jāti.*
2. This *jāti* does not belong to me.
3. The *jāti* is superimposition on the gross body.
4. I, the knower of this *jāti* like the knower of pot, am different from it.

Such a *jāti* is not me and not mine. This is to be understood.

Q. 53: "The *āśrama* is not me and not mine", how to know this?

Ans: 1. *Brahmacārī, gṛhastha, vānaprastha* and *saṁnyāsī* — these four stages are superimposed on the gross body for the sake of performance of different actions.

2. It is not the attribute of the human being.

Therefore,

1. I am not this *āśrama.*
2. This *āśrama* is not mine.

3. This *āśrama* is a superimposition on the gross body.
4. I, the knower of these *āśrama*s like the knower of pot, am different from these.

Such an *āśrama* is not me and not mine. This is to be understood.

Q. 54: "The *varṇa* also known as colour is not me and not mine". How to know this?

Ans: 1. White, green, red, yellow, etc. are colours. It is the quality of the gross body which is perceived directly.

2. I am not the gross body.

Therefore,

1. I am not this colour.
2. This colour is not mine.
3. The colour belongs to the gross body.
4. I, the knower of these colours like the knower of pot, am different from it.

I am not such a colour, and it is not mine. This is to be known.

Q. 55: "Relation is not me and not mine", how to understand this?

Ans: 1. Relations like father–son, teacher–disciple, wife–husband and master–servant are mutually well known from the standpoint of the gross body which is false.

2. On analysis, such relations are not attained.

3. I am without relation, being different from the gross body.

Therefore,

1. I am not this relation.
2. This relation is not mine.
3. This relation is superimposed on the gross body.
4. I, the knower of these relations like the knower of pot, am different from these.

Such a relation is not me and not mine. This is to be known.

Q. 56: "The 'modification' that assumes a form is not me and not mine", how to know this?

Ans: 1. Long, short, thin, fat, straight, crooked such forms are from the standpoint of the gross body.

2. I am formless and different from the gross body.

Therefore,

1. I am not this form.
2. This form is not me.
3. This form is from the standpoint of the gross body.
4. I, the knower of this form like the knower of pot, am different from it.

Such a form is not me and not mine. This is to be known.

Q. 57: "I am not subject to birth and death, and birth or death does not occur to me", how to know this? [See also Q. 158.]

Ans: [1] If *ātmā* is said to be born then *ātmā* will be non-eternal. This is the view of Mīmāṁsā who are *āstika*s with a belief in the other world. For them this [non-eternity of *ātmā*] is not acceptable. It is said if *ātmā* is subject to origination then it will be subject to destruction. Then,

1. there may be the experience of happiness and sorrow as results of actions not done in the previous birth and
2. the action done in this birth will be destroyed without experiencing [its results].

These are the two defects that may occur. According to *karmavādin*, *ātmā* is to be known as doer and reaper. Then too, *ātmā* as devoid of birth and death is to be known.

[2] And there is no possibility of indicating the cause for the origin of *ātmā*. It is said that the cause of *ātmā* is to be different from *ātmā* and

1. that which is different from *ātmā* is *anātmā* name and form. Since the cause cannot be determined, *ātmā* is to be imagined as in the case of rope-snake.
2. *Brahman* is non-different from *ātmā* like the total space which is non-different from pot space. So, *Brahman* cannot be the cause.

Therefore there is no birth for *ātmā*.

[3] When *ātmā* is not subject to birth then there is no death for *ātmā*.

[4] Thus, in *ātmā* there is the absence of birth and death. Then *ātmā* is free from birth, existence, growth, modification, decaying and death. *Ātmā* is devoid of these six modifications.

Therefore,

1. I am not subject to birth and death.
2. Birth and death cannot occur to me.
3. Birth and death are because of action done by the gross body.
4. I, the knower of birth and death like the knower of pot, am different from birth and death.

In this manner I am not subject to birth and death, and in me birth and death cannot happen. This is to be known.

Q. 58: What is the example of elimination of the five great elements?

Ans: For example, it is like as if one is possessed by a ghost. A person is called upon to ward off the ghost. He plays the *ḍamaru*, prepares a mixture with five ingredients like salt etc. and offers to ward off the ghost.

Application: The five great elements becoming the gross body possess the *jīva*. To remove this, one approaches a *brahmaniṣṭha guru* as enjoined[52] and take refuge. The teaching of the Vedic scripture is like playing of the *ḍamaru*. Each of the five aspects under the twenty-five principles mentioned above is offered to its respective elements. I am the seer of these twenty-five principles. In this manner, it is ascertained and there is the absolute cessation[53] of the five great elements. In this way, know that, I am the witness of the gross body.

2. I Am the Witness of the Subtle Body

Q. 59: What is subtle body?

Ans: That which is made of ungrossified five elements with seventeen sense-organs is known as the subtle body.

Q. 60: What are the seventeen sense-organs of the subtle body?

Ans: (1-5) Five sense-organs of knowledge, (6-10) five sense-organs of action, (11-15) five airs, (16) mind and (17) intellect. These are the seventeen sense-organs.

Q. 61: What are the five sense-organs of knowledge?[54]

Ans: (1-5) Sense of hearing, touch, sight, taste and smell. These are the five sense-organs of knowledge.

---

52 With the qualities like discrimination, desirous of liberation, an *adhikārī*:

(1) takes refuge at the feet of the teacher with [appropriate] offerings,

(2) prostrates, touching the eight limbs on the floor.

(3) "O Lord! Please instruct me the knowledge of *Brahman*" saying this, "what is bondage? what is liberation? what is ignorance? and what is knowledge?" such questions are raised. And

(4) surrenders totally — body, mind, wealth, speech and engages in the service of the *guru*.

This is the injunction for gaining self-knowledge.

53 That which does not occur again is known as absolute cessation.

54 Sense-organs instrumental for gaining knowledge are sense-organs of knowledge.

Q. 62: What are the five organs of action?[55]

Ans: (6-10) Speech, hand, feet, reproductive and excretory organ. These are the five sense-organs of action.

Q. 63: What are the five airs?

Ans: (11-15) *Prāṇa, apāna, samāna, udāna* and *vyāna*. These are the five airs.

Q. 64: What is mind?

Ans: The thought that is of indecisive nature. It is known as the mind.

Q. 65: What is intellect?

Ans: The thought that is of decisive nature. It is known as the intellect.

Q. 66: What is meant by non-grossified five elements?

Ans: Those elements which have not undergone the process of grossification in earlier stage.

1. It can be said as non-grossified five elements.
2. It is known as subtle element.
3. It is also known as *tanmātras*.

Q. 67: How are the non-grossified five elements with seventeen organs to be known?

Ans: The content of five organs of knowledge and action

1. The *sattva*[56] aspect of space is the sense of hearing.
2. The *rajas* aspect of space is speech.

    [1] The sense of hearing, hears the words.

    [2] The sense of speech, speaks the words.

---

55 Sense-organs instrumental for performance of action are sense-organs of action.

56 The three qualities *sattva, rajas* and *tamas* are present in all entities.

Therefore,

[1] Sense of hearing is an organ of knowledge.

[2] Sense of speech is an organ of action.

These two are associated.

3. The *sattva* aspect of air is sense of touch. And
4. the *rajas* aspect of air is hand (sense of grasping etc.).

[1] The sense of touch (skin), knows touch.

[2] The hand grasps things.

Therefore,

[1] Sense of touch is an organ of knowledge.

[2] Hand is an organ of action.

These two are associated.

5. The *sattva* aspect of fire is sense of sight. And
6. the *rajas* aspect of fire is feet (locomotion).

[1] The sense of sight grasps the colour.

[2] The feet moves.

Therefore,

[1] Sense of sight is an organ of knowledge.

[2] Feet is an organ of action.

These two are associated.

7. The *sattva* aspect of water is sense of taste.
8. The *rajas* aspect of water is reproductive organ.

[1] The tongue senses taste.

[2] The reproductive organ releases liquid.

Therefore,

[1] Sense of taste is an organ of knowledge.

[2] Reproductive organ is an organ of action.

These two are associated.

9. The *sattva* aspect of earth is sense of smell.
10. The *rajas* aspect of earth is excretory organ.

[1] The sense of smell grasps smell.

[2] The excretory organ removes smell (waste).

Therefore,

[1] Sense of smell is an organ of knowledge.

[2] Excretory organ is an organ of action.

These two are associated.

Five Airs, Mind and Intellect

(11-15) The total *rajas* aspects of the five elements put together are five airs.

(16-17) The total *sattva* aspect of the five elements is the internal organ. This internal organ is referred to as mind and intellect. Here, the memory and ego are included in mind and intellect.

These seventeen organs are the products of the non-grossified elements.

Q. 68: What is the benefit of knowing these seventeen sense-organs?

Ans: These seventeen sense-organs are not me and they are not mine. They belong to the non-grossified elements. This is the benefit of knowing the seventeen organs.

Q. 69: For what reason should one know that these seventeen sense-organs are not me and not mine?

Ans: I am the knower of these seventeen sense-organs. One who knows an entity is different from that entity. This is the law. By this reason, I am not these seventeen sense-organs and they are not mine. This is to be known.

Q. 70: What is the example in this regard?

Ans: Example: [1] The dancing hall [2] lamp [3] king [4] minister [5] attendants [6] heroine [7] instrumentalists, and [8] people in the hall [9] when they are seated they are illumined [10] when all go away then also the empty hall is illumined.

Explanation: In the same way, [1] the gross body in the form of dancing hall [2] the witness consciousness like the lamp [3] the reflected consciousness in the form of king [4] the minister like the mind [5] the five vital airs like the attendants [6] the intellect like the heroine [7] the ten sense-organs in the form of instrumentalists [8] the sense-objects in the form of sound, etc. like the people in the hall [9] in waking and dream states these are illumined [10] in deep sleep these are absent, this absence is also illumined.

In this case, this is to be taken as the apt example.

Q. 71: How is this to be understood?

Ans: 1. During waking state, with the help of both the sense-organs and the internal organ I am luminous and I know.

2. In dream state, without the sense-organs and with only the internal organ, I am luminous.

3. In deep sleep state, without the aid of either the sense-organs or the internal organ, I alone am luminous. Know in this manner.

Q. 72: What is the example in this regard?

Ans: Example: Just as [1] within a pot with five holes there is a lamp with oil and thread. [2] That lamp-light illumines the lamp-pot, oil, thread and the internal parts of the pot and illumining the holes of the pot; the beams pass through the holes and illumine the external objects like the flower-vase and bunch of flowers. All these are illumined by the light piercing out through the hole. [3] The sunlight illumines the whole universe. And [4] the powerful light in its general form is all-pervasive.

Explanation: [1] The five sense-organs of knowledge are like the five holes in the pot, and the gross body is like the pot, inside the body is the lotus-heart in the form of a vessel. In it is the mind likened to oil and intellect like the thread. In it is the Self which is the light. [2] The lotus-heart vessel, oil like mind, thread like intellect and the internal parts of the body and the holes like the sense-organs are known, illumined. The sensory objects like sound etc., through the sense-organs are also illumined. [3] The entire universe is illumined by *Īśvara.* [4] The general consciousness in the form of *Brahman* is all-pervasive. This is the example[57] in this case.

Q. 73: By this what gets established?

Ans: By this it is understood that I am not the seventeen sense-organs and the seventeen sense-organs are not me. They belong to the five great elements. I am the knower by witnessing them, like the seer of pot, I am different from these. This gets established.

Q. 74: "I am not the seventeen sense-organs and the seventeen sense-organs are not in me", how to know this?

Ans: (1-5) Five Sense-organs of Knowledge:

1. Sense of hearing

    [1] I hear the sound; that is I know sound, and

    [2] if sound is not heard, I know the absence of sound.

Thus, I am not the sense of hearing and the sense of hearing is not mine. It belongs to space. I am its knower as the seer of pot, am different from it.

2. Sense of touch

    [1] I am aware of touch, and

    [2] If there is no touch, I know the absence of touch.

Thus, I am not the sense of touch and the sense of touch is not mine. It belongs to air. I am its knower as the seer of pot, am different from it.

---

57 There is an example of a sacrificial ground. It is discussed in the seventh digit in the context of describing *ātmā* in the form of onlooker [see Q. 151.].

3. Sense of sight

   [1] I am aware of colours, and

   [2] if the colour is not seen, I know the absence of colour.

Thus, I am not the sense of sight and the sense of sight is not mine. It belongs to fire. I am its knower as the seer of pot, am different from it.

4. Sense of taste

   [1] I am aware of taste, and

   [2] if there is no taste, I know the absence of taste.

Thus, I am not the sense of taste and the sense of taste is not mine. It belongs to water. I am its knower as the seer of pot, am different from it.

5. Sense of smell

   [1] I am aware of smell, and

   [2] if there is no smell, I know the absence of smell.

Thus, I am not the sense of smell and the sense of smell is not mine. It belongs to earth. I am its knower as the seer of pot, am different from it.

(6-10) Five Sense-organs of Action:

6. Sense of speech

   [1] speech is known to me and

   [2] if there is no speech, its absence is also known to me.

Thus, I am not the sense of speech and the sense of speech is not mine. It belongs to space. I am its knower as the seer of pot, am different from it.

7. Sense of grasping (hands)

   [1] giving and taking are known to me, and

   [2] if it is not done, its absence is also known to me.

Thus, I am not the hand and the hand is not mine. It belongs to air. I am its knower as the seer of pot, am different from it.

8. Sense of locomotion (legs)

   [1] Movement is known to me, and

   [2] if there is no movement, its absence is also known to me.

Thus, I am not the leg and the leg is not mine. It belongs to fire. I am its knower as the seer of pot, am different from it.

9. Sense-organ of reproduction

   [1] The release of liquid (urine and *vīrya*) I know, and

   [2] when it is not released, its absence is also known to me.

Thus, I am not the sense-organ of reproduction and it is not mine. It belongs to water. I am its knower as the seer of pot, am different from it.

10. Sense-organ of excretion

   [1] I know the evacuation of solid waste, and

   [2] if not evacuated, its absence is also known to me.

Thus, I am not the sense-organ of excretion and it is not mine. It belongs to earth. I am its knower as the seer of pot, am different from it.

(11-17) Vital Air and Internal Organ

11-15. Five airs:

   [1] Action done is known to me, and

   [2] when there is no action, its absence is also known to me.

Thus, I am not the vital airs and the vital airs are not mine. They belong to the total five great elements. I am their knower as the seer of pot, am different from them.

16. Mind

[1] Resolution (*saṅkalpa*) and alternatives (*vikalpa*) are known to me, and

[2] when resolutions and alternatives are not done, their absence is also known to me.

Thus, I am not the mind and the mind is not mine. It belongs to the total five great elements. I am its knower as the seer of pot, am different from it.

17. Intellect

[1] The conviction is known to me, and

[2] when there is no conviction, its absence is also known to me.

Thus, I am not the intellect and the intellect is not mine. It belongs to the total five great elements. I am its knower as the seer of pot, am different from it.

In this manner, the seventeen sense-organs are not me and the seventeen sense-organs are not mine. This is to be understood.

Q. 75: What is the purpose of this knowledge?

Ans: 1. Doer is the subtle body and its features of merits and demerits, whose results in the form of pleasure and pain is experienced. And

2. there is travel in this world and to the other world, and

3. the *sāttvika* thoughts like dispassion, mind control and sense control, and *rājasika* thoughts like attachment, hatred and delight and *tāmasika* thoughts like sleep, laziness and negligence,

4. hunger, thirst, blindness, etc., and dullness and intelligence.

I am not these and these are not mine. This conviction is gained.

Q. 76: How is that I am not the doer of good and bad, and not the reaper of results of pleasure and pain and how are the qualities doership and enjoyership not me? How to know this?

Ans: (1) That which is subject to change can do and is the doer. I am changeless, stable and am not the locus of action. So, I am not the doer of merits or demerits. And a non-doer is not a reaper. It is the attribute of the mind. It is not mine. I am its knower as the seer of pot, am different from it. It should be known in this manner.

Q. 77: The appearance and disappearance from this world and into the other world is not my attribute. How to know this?

Ans: (2) The mind (subtle body) is limited. The appearance and disappearance of this subtle body are based on fructified results (*prārabdha karma*) and I am all-pervasive like the space. My attribute is not that of appearing and disappearing. This should be known in this way.

Q. 78: "I am not the *sāttvika, rājasika* and *tāmasika* thoughts and they are not my attributes." How to know this?

Ans: (3) Like in the example, [1] in a certain palace is seated a [2] king, for whose amusement, [3] some craftsperson [4] brings a fruit [5] by opening the tender part of the fruit, there flows three streaks of water [6] within the three streaks there are manifold flows [7] when the tender part is closed, the three streams get closed and there remains the king alone.

Explanation: in the same way [1] the gross body is like the palace [2] the substratum unchanging consciousness is the king, for whose delight [3] *māyā* (ignorance) in the form of the craftsperson [4] the internal organ as the fruit [5] the *prārabdha* fructifies through the waking and dream states, the three streaks are the three *guṇa*s that flow out. [6] in the three streaks there emerges manifold thoughts [7] when *prārabdha* does not fructify in deep-sleep state, the presence and absence of thoughts are illumined by consciousness, king who alone remains. That is Me. But, the *sāttvika, rājasika* or *tāmasika* thoughts are not Me.

They belong to the mind. I am its knower as the seer of pot, am different from it. It should be known in this manner.

Q. 79: "The blindness, dull-wittedness and intelligence are not me and are not my attributes." How to know this?

Ans: (4) [1] The sense-organ of sight that does not grasp its sense object is blindness. I am aware of this.

[2] If the sense object is grasped vaguely it is dull-wittedness. I am the knower of this.

[3] If the sense object is grasped completely it is known as intelligence. I am the knower of this.

Thus, they are not me and they are not mine. They are the attributes of the sense-organs. I am its knower as the seer of pot, am different from it. It should be known in this manner.

In this way, I am the witness of the subtle body.

3. I Am the Witness of the Causal Body

Q. 80: What is causal body?

Ans: 1. On waking up from deep sleep, a person says "I did not know anything", this is said to be ignorance in deep sleep.[58] This is established. And

2. in the waking state, there are expressions like "I do not know *Brahman*"and "I do not know this". The content of these experiences is ignorance. And

3. the cause of dream is ignorance in the form of sleep.

This ignorance is causal body.[59]

---

[58] A person waking up from deep sleep says "I did not know anything", such a knowledge takes place. This knowledge is not experienced but it is the experience of ignorance in deep-sleep state that is remembered.

The content of this memory is the ignorance in deep-sleep state.

[59] (1) Ignorance is the cause of gross and subtle bodies. Therefore, →

Q. 81: "I am not the causal body and it is not mine". How to know this?

Ans: "I know" and "I don't know" are the thoughts in the mind. They are known along with the content of knowing and not knowing. I am not this causal body and it is not mine. It belongs to ignorance.[60] I am its knower as the seer of pot, am different from it. It should be known in this manner.

In this manner I am the witness of the causal body.

Thus ends the third digit of *Vicāracandrodaya* titled "I Am the Witness of the Three Bodies".

→ it is known as the cause of these two bodies.

(2) By self-knowledge, this ignorance is destroyed and hence it is called as "body".

This ignorance like the darkness in the *sanctum-sanctorum* of a temple, located in *Brahman*, conceals *Brahman*.

60 The causal body is ignorance. It is said as "it is of ignorance". It is like referring to Rāhu itself as head of Rāhu. In the same way [the causal body is referred to as ignorance of ignorance].

Kalā 4

I Am Beyond the Five Sheaths

मनहर छंद (*Manahara* Metre)

पंचकोशातीत मैं हूं अन्न प्राण मनोमय।
विज्ञान आनंदमय पंचकोश नातमा।।

स्थूलदेह अन्नमय-कोश लिंगदेह प्राण-
मन रु विज्ञान तीनकोश कहें मातमा।।

कारण आनंदमय-कोश ये कारज जड।
विकारी विनाशी व्यभिचारीहीं अनातमा।

अज चित अविकारी नित्य व्यभिचारहीन।
पीतांबर अनुभव करता मैं आतमा।। ४ ।।

pañcakośātīta maiṁ hūṁ anna prāṇa manomaya।
vijñāna ānandamaya pañcakośa nātamā।।

sthūladeha annamaya-kośa liṅgadeha prāṇa-
mana ru vijñāna tīnakośa kaheṁ mātamā।।

kāraṇa ānandamaya-kośa ye kāraja jaḍa।
vikārī vināśī vyabhicārīhīṁ anātamā।

aja cita avikārī nitya vyabhicārahīna।
pītāṁbara anubhava karatā maiṁ ātamā।। 4 ।।

I transcend the five-sheaths, *annamaya, prāṇamaya, manomaya,*
vijñānamaya and *ānandamaya* are the five sheaths which are non-self.[61]

The gross body is food-sheath, the subtle body[62] is vital air, mental and intellect sheaths which are non-self.

---

61 (Non-self) means it is not *ātmā*, i.e. it is *anātmā*.

62 The subtle body constitutes the three *kośas* — *prāṇamaya, manomaya* and *vijñānamaya*.

The causal body is bliss-sheath[63] which is inert
non-self is subject to modification, destruction and change.
Self experienced (known) by Pitambar is Birthless, Consciousness Unmodifying, Eternal and Changeless || 4 ||

Q. 82: What is meant by transcendence of the five sheaths?

Ans: Transcendence of the five sheaths means I am different and beyond the five sheaths.

Q. 83: What is meant by "sheath"?

Ans: 1. Sheath is the name of the cover of a sword,

2. store-house of treasure and

3. the dwelling place of a [certain] worm.

Like these, the five sheaths conceal the Self. Therefore, the *annamaya* etc. are called as the sheaths.

Q. 84: What are the names of the five sheaths?

Ans: (1) *Annamaya kośa*, (2) *prāṇamaya kośa*, (3) *manomaya kośa*, (4) *vijñānamaya kośa* and (5) *ānandamaya kośa*. These are the names of the five sheaths.

Q. 85: What is *annamaya kośa*?

Ans: 1. The food consumed by mother and father gets converted into the male seed in the father which is the cause for conception in the mother.

2. Then, the milk etc. consumed as food by the child after birth.

3. After death the body resolves into the earth, the giver of food.

This is the gross body which is called *annamaya kośa*.

Q. 86: How is that *annamaya kośa*?

Ans: It is the abode of the experience of happiness and sorrow.

---

[63] One of the five sheaths.

Q. 87: "I am different from *annamaya kośa*", how should one know it?

Ans: 1. *Annamaya kośa* was non-existent prior to birth and will be non-existent posterior to death. There is the non-existence of the gross body. Since it is subject to origination and destruction like a pot, it is an effect. And

2. I am always of the nature of Existence. Since I am free from origination and destruction I am beyond the gross body.

I am not this *annamaya kośa* and the *annamaya kośa* is not mine. It is of the nature of gross body. I am the knower of the physical body hence I am different from it. In this way, one should know that I am beyond *annamaya kośa*.

Q. 88: What is *prāṇamaya kośa*?

Ans: The five *prāṇa*s along with five sense-organs of action are known as *prāṇamaya kośa*.

Q. 89: What are the five sense-organs of action and five vital airs?

Ans: The sense-organs of action and the five vital airs have been enumerated in the earlier section under subtle body. [See Qs. 62 and 63.]

Q. 90: What are the position and function of the five vital airs?

Ans: 1. Respiration (*prāṇa vāyu*).

[1] Its position is the heart.

[2] Everyday it carries out the function of inhalation and exhalation for 21,600 times.

2. Evacuation (*apāna vāyu*)

[1] The sense-organ of excretion is its position.

[2] Its function is to evacuate liquid and solid wastes from the body.

3. Digestive (*samāna vāyu*)

[1] Its position is in the navel.

[2] Its activity is to digest the food consumed so that the essence of the food consumed reaches the entire body through the *nāḍīs* just like a gardener who waters the garden with the water drawn from a well.

4. Reversal (*udāna vāyu*)

[1] Its position is the neck region.

[2] It separates the consumed food and water; and its activity is to project a dream.

5. Circulation (*vyāna vāyu*)

[1] Its position is the entire body.

[2] Its function is to circulate (blood, essence of food) in the entire body.

In this manner we find the location and activity of the five *prāṇas*.

Q. 91: What is the function of *prāṇa*, etc. with respect to the body?

Ans: The *prāṇa* etc.,

1. through their function in the entire body give strength to the body.
2. they serve as the means to perform the respective function of each sense-organ.

Q. 92: "I am different from *prāṇamaya kośa*". How to know this?

Ans: When a person is sleeping, the *prāṇa* is awake.

1. Even then, when a friend arrives, the person (who is sleeping) does not welcome him.
2. When a thief takes away valuables, the (sleeping) person does not stop him.

Thus, this *prāṇa vāyu* is inert like a pot and I am Consciousness different from it. This *prāṇamaya kośa* is not me and it is not mine. It is part of the subtle body. I am the knower of this and hence different from it. In this way, I am different from *prāṇamaya kośa*. This is to be known.

Q. 93: What is *manomaya kośa*?

Ans: The mind with the five sense-organs of knowledge is known as *manomaya kośa*.

Q. 94: What are the five sense-organs of knowledge and mind?

Ans: These were said earlier in the context of subtle body. [See Qs. 61 and 64].

Q. 95: What is mind?

Ans: Mind is in the form of "I" identifying with the body and because of identification with house, etc., it is in the form of "mine", it travels through the sense-organs and is of the nature of cause.

Q. 96: "I am different from *manomaya kośa*". How to know this?

Ans:
1. Since there are thought-modifications in the form of desire, anger, etc., the mind is not confined to an order and is subject to change.
2. I am the witness of all thoughts and am changeless. Thus I am not the *manomaya kośa* and it is not mine. It belongs to the subtle body. I am the knower of it and hence different from it. In this manner, I am different from *manomaya kośa*. This is to be known.

Q. 97: What is *vijñānamaya kośa*?

Ans: The intellect along with five sense-organs of knowledge is *vijñānamaya kośa*.

Q. 98: What are the sense-organs of knowledge and intellect?

Ans: This has been mentioned earlier in the context of subtle body. [See Qs. 61 and 65.]

Q. 99: What is intellect?

Ans: 1. In deep sleep, the intellect with the reflected consciousness[64] resolves.

2. During waking state, it pervades from the tip of the nail up to the head, in the entire body in the form of doer.

Q. 100: "I am different from *vijñānamaya kośa*". How to know this?

Ans: 1. The intellect like pot is subject to the state of resolution and hence is destructible.

2. I am not subject to states like resolution, am different and indestructible.

This *vijñānamaya kośa* is not me and it is not mine. It belongs to the subtle body. I am the knower of it. In this way, I am different from *vijñānamaya kośa*. This is to be known.

Q. 101: What is *ānandamaya kośa*?

Ans: 1. In the experience of the fructification of result of merit (*puṇya*) at times, the thought in the intellect becomes inward in which there is the reflection of *ānanda* which is the nature of Self.

2. It is known as *priya, moda* and *pramoda.*

3. At the end of experience of the result of merit, this thought resolves in sleep.

That thought is known as *ānandamaya kośa.*

Q. 102: How is this *ānandamaya kośa*?

Ans: 1. The rise of *priya* thought on seeing a desired object is its "head".

---

64 (1) Just as the brilliance of light and space seems non-different but [actually] they are different.

(2) Just as the hot iron piece and fire seems non-different but [actually] they are different.

Similarly, the internal organ and Self seems non-different but [actually] they are different. During deep sleep when the internal organ resolves, the Self remains as the witness of ignorance.

2. By obtaining the desired object there is *moda* thought which is its one (right) "wing".
3. By the experience of the obtained desired object there is *pramoda* thought which is its other (left) "wing".
4. Its nature is of the reflection of *ānanda* of Self in the form of intellect and ignorance.
5. The nature of Self is original *ānanda* which forms its "tail"[65] (substratum).

Such an experiencer in the form of (imagined as) a bird is *ānandamaya kośa*.[66]

Q. 103: "I am different from *ānandamaya kośa*". How to know this?

Ans: 1. *Ānandamaya kośa* is that which occurs like cloud in a particular time. It is momentary.

2. I am always immovable and eternal.

I am not this *ānandamaya kośa* and it is not mine. It belongs to the causal body. I am the knower of it and hence different from it. In this way I am different from *ānandamaya kośa*. This is to be known.

Q. 104: If the available five sheaths are not Self then what is Self?

Ans: 1. That which remains as intellect due to reflection

2. and which is referred to by names like *priya*. Such an *ānandamaya kośa* whose cause is the original (*bimba*) *ānanda*, is eternal which is the Self.

---

65 Since the substratum is *ānanda* which is the nature of *Brahman*, the *Taittirīya Upaniṣad* uses the word "tail" [in the sense of substratum or support].

66 In this manner, the other four *kośa*s are presented in the form of a bird which is elaborately discussed in the Hindi commentary to *Taittirīya Upaniṣad* [by Pitambar]. Those who are interested can refer to it.

Q. 105: The five sheaths alone are subject to experience. Other than these sheaths, there is no experience in Self. That is, Self is different from the five sheaths. How to achieve conviction in this?

Ans: Even though the five sheaths alone are subject to experience, other than these the Self does not experience, this is true, then also, through experience these five sheaths are known, who will remove such an experience? No one else can remove this experience.

Thus, the Consciousness in the form of experience in the five sheaths is Self which is different from the five sheaths.

Q. 106: How is this Self?

Ans: Self is of the nature of Existence, Consciousness, Absolute Happiness.

Thus ends the fourth digit of *Vicāracandrodaya* titled "I Am Beyond the Five Sheaths".

Kalā 5

I Am the Witness of the Three States

मनहर छंद (*Manahara* Metre)

अवस्था तीनको साक्षी आतमा अन्वय याको।
व्यभिचारीअवस्थाको व्यतिरेक पाईयो।।

त्रिपुटी चतुरदश करि व्यवहार जहां।
स्पष्ट सो जाग्रत् जूठ ताकूं दृश्य ध्याईयो।।

देखे सुने वस्तुनके संस्कारसैं सृष्टि जहां।
अस्पष्टप्रतीति स्वप्न मृषा लोक गाईयो।।

सकलकरण लय होय जहां सुषुप्ति सो।
पीतांबर तुरीयहीं प्रत्यक प्रत्याईयो।। ५ ।।

avasthā tīnako sākṣī ātamā anvaya yāko ।
vyabhicārī avasthāko vyatireka pāīyo ।।

tripuṭī caturadaśa kari vyavahāra jahāṅ ।
spaṣṭa so jāgrat jūṭha tākūṅ dṛśya dhyāīyo ।।

dekhe sune vastunake saṁskārasaiṅ sṛṣṭi jahāṅ ।
aspaṣṭapratīti svapna mṛṣā loka gāīyo ।।

sakalakaraṇa laya hoya jahāṅ suṣupti so ।
pītāṁbara turīyahīṅ pratyaka pratyāīyo ।। 5 ।।

The witness of the three states, the Self is inherent[67] and the varying states are obtained differently.[68]

---

67 "Immanent" means that which is like the thread of a garland inherent in the three states.

68 Like the flowers in a garland, the three states are mutually different and are also different from the substratum.

Where the interaction consists of fourteen triads
is evident in the waking state which is false, is perceived.

From the seen, heard things, impressions create
a vague dream which is a false world.

All instruments resolve where,[69] is deep sleep
Pitambar is *turīya* — the inner[70] is declared[71] ॥ 5 ॥

Q. 107: What are the three states of experiences?

Ans: (1) Waking state,[72] (2) dream state[73] and (3) deep-sleep state.[74] These are the three states of experiences.

1. I Am the Witness of Waking State

Q. 108: What is waking state?

Ans: 1. Fourteen senses are *adhyātma*.[75]

2. The corresponding fourteen presiding deities are *adhideva*.[76]

---

69 This is to be read as — where all instruments resolve that is deep sleep.

70 The inner self.

71 Ascertained.

72 That which is different from dream and deep-sleep states and is the base for the knowledge gained by sense-organs and the impressions caused by the knowledge gained by the sense-organs, is the waking state.

73 Dream state is that in which the knowledge is not produced by the sense-organs and the sense objects perceived [in dream] are direct thought of the internal organ.

74 Deep-sleep state is that in which the thought pertaining to ignorance and happiness is experienced.

75 *Adhyātma* is that which has *ātmā* as its substratum because of which the sense-organs function.

76 That which is different from its own composition and is not the object of perception through the sense of sight is known as *Adhideva*.

3. The corresponding fourteen sense objects are *adhibhūta*.[77]

All these when involved in interaction (*vyavahāra*) is known as the waking state.[78]

Q. 109: What are the fourteen sense-organs?

Ans: (1-5) *Sense-organs of knowledge*: (1) sense of hearing, (2) sense of touch, (3) sense of sight, (4) sense of taste, and (5) sense of smell.

(6-10) *Sense-organs of action*: (6) sense of speech, (7) sense of grasp, etc. (hand), (8) sense of locomotion (leg), (9) sense-organ of evacuation (excretion), and (10) sense-organ of reproduction.

(11-14) *Internal sense-organ*: (11) mind, (12) intellect, (13) memory, and (14) self-identification.

These fourteen sense-organs are *adhyātma*.

Q. 110: What are the corresponding fourteen presiding deities for the fourteen sense-organs?

Ans: [1-5] Presiding deities of the five sense-organs of knowledge

1. The deities of directions (*dikpāla*s) preside the sense of hearing.
2. Vāyu presides the sense-organ of touch.
3. Sūrya presides over the sense of sight.
4. Varuṇa presides over the sense of taste.
5. Aśvinīkumāras presides the sense of smell.

[6-10] Presiding deities of the sense-organ of action:

6. Agni presides over the sense of speech.
7. Indra presides over the sense of grasp etc. (hand).
8. Vāmana presides over the sense of locomotion.

---

77 This is different from its composition and is perceptible by the sense of sight etc. is known as *Adhibhūta*.

78 The characteristic of waking state is that which is capable of perceiving through the gross sense-organs and knows the experiences of dream and deep-sleep states.

9. Yama presides over sense of evacuation.
10. Prajāpati presides over the sense of reproduction.

[11-14] Presiding deities of the internal sense-organ:[79]

11. Candra is the deity of mind.
12. The deity of intellect is Brahmā.
13. Vāsudeva presides over memory.
14. Rudra presides over self-identification.

These fourteen deities are *adhidevas*.

Q. 111: What are the fourteen sense objects corresponding to the fourteen sense-organs?

Ans: [1-5] The sense objects of five sense-organs of knowledge are:

1. sound
2. touch
3. colour
4. taste
5. smell.

[6-10] The sense objects of five senses of action are:

6. words
7. grasping
8. walking
9. removal of waste
10. pleasure.

[11-14] The sense objects of the internal organ are:

11. resolve–alternation (indecisive function)[80]
12. decisive function

---

[79] Internal organ is in the form of sense-organ within.

[80] The resolve–alternation is not the sense object of mind but the object based on which the resolve is carried out is said to be the sense object of mind. In the same way, understand intellect, memory, self identification and the sense-organs of action.

13. recollection
14. notion of "I".

These are the fourteen sense objects known as *adhibhūtas*.

Q. 112: What is the combination of these three — *adhyātma, adhidaiva* and *adhibhūta* — known as?

Ans: The combination of these three together is called a triad (*tripuṭī*).

Q. 113: How to understand these fourteen triads?

Ans: (1-5) The triad of the sense-organs of knowledge

	Sense-organ (*Adhyātma*)	Presiding Deity (*Adhideva*)	Sense Object (*Adhibhūta*)
[1]	Sense of hearing	Dik	Sound
[2]	Sense of touch	Vāyu	Touch
[3]	Sense of sight	Sūrya	Colour
[4]	Sense of taste	Varuṇa	Taste
[5]	Sense of smell	Aśvinīkumāras	Smell

(6-10) The triad of sense-organ of action

	Sense-organ (*Adhyātma*)	Presiding Deity (*Adhideva*)	Sense object (*Adhibhūta*)
[6]	Sense of speech	Agni	Words
[7]	Sense of grasp	Indra	Giving–taking
[8]	Sense of locomotion	Vāmana	Movement
[9]	Sense of reproduction	Prajāpati	Pleasure
[10]	Sense of evacuation	Yama	Removal of wastes

(11-14) The triad of the fourfold internal sense-organ

[11]	Mind	Candra	Resolve–alternation
[12]	Intellect	Brahmā	Firm
[13]	Memory	Vāsudeva	Recollection
[14]	Self-identification	Rudra	Notion of "I"

In this way, know the fourteen triads.

Q. 114: What are the natures of these fourteen triads?

Ans: The triad consists of three aspects, of which even if one is absent the respective transaction does not take place. For example:

1. The sense-organ and presiding deity are present but the sense object is not there, then transaction (*vyavahāra*) does not take place.
2. Sense object and sense-organs are present without the [blessing of the] presiding deity, then too transaction does not take place.

In this way, the entire triad is to be known.

Q. 115: How to know my nature?

Ans: 1. I know when the triad is complete.

2. I know when the triad is incomplete.
3. I know the transactions through the triad.
4. I know the absence of transactions.

This is my nature. This is to be known.

Q. 116: By this what gets established?

Ans: The mode of transaction that happens through the triad is the waking state. This gets established.

Q. 117: What is the location, kind of speech, experience, power, quality of the individual in the waking state and what is the name of the individual in the waking state?

Ans: The individual in the waking state has:

1. The eye[81] as the location.
2. *Vaikharī* is the kind of speech.
3. Experience is gross.
4. Power is action.

---

[81] Even though in waking state the individual in the form of reflected consciousness pervades the entire body from tip of nail to head, then also, the primary position is said to be the "eye" and hence the location of the individual in the waking state is said to be the "eye".

5. Quality is *rajas*.
6. By the identification with the waking state the individual is known as *viśva*.

Q. 118: What gets established from the waking state?

Ans: 1. The waking state is known by Me.

2. The absence of dream and deep-sleep states is also known by Me.

I am not the waking state and it is not mine. It belongs to the gross body. I am the knower and witness of it as that of a pot. In this way, I am the witness of the waking state.

2. I Am the Witness of Dream State

Q. 119: What is dream state?

Ans: In the waking state, the objects are perceived, heard, experienced and these impressions are located in the neck region in the *nāḍīs* called *hita* which are minute like a piece of hair cut into thousand parts. During sleep, the five senses and sense objects get projected by which transaction takes place. This is dream state.

Q. 120: What is the location, kind of speech, experience, power, quality of the individual in the dream state and what is the name of the individual in the dream state?

Ans: The individual in the dream state has:

1. The neck region as the location.
2. *Madhyamā* is the kind of speech.
3. Experience is subtle (of impressions).
4. Power is knowledge.
5. Quality is *sattva*.[82]
6. By the identification with the dream state the individual is known as *taijasa*.

---

[82] Some say, *rajas* is the quality.

Q. 121: What gets established through dream state?

Ans: 1. The dream state is known to Me.

2. The absence of waking and deep-sleep states are known to Me.

This dream state is not me and it is not mine. It belongs to the subtle body. I am the knower and witness of it as that of a pot. This gets established by the dream state. In this way, I am the witness of the dream state.

3. I Am the Witness of Deep-sleep State

Q. 122: What is deep-sleep state?

Ans: A person, on waking up, recollects the experience of bliss and ignorance in deep sleep and expresses as "I slept happily" and "I did not know anything". This bliss and ignorance are illumined by the witness consciousness that is experienced. This resolved state of intellect is said to be the deep-sleep state.

Q. 123: What are the location, kind of speech, experience, power, quality of the individual in the deep-sleep state and what is the name of the individual in the deep-sleep state?

Ans: The individual in the deep-sleep state has

1. The heart as the location.
2. *Paśyantī* is the kind of speech.
3. Experience is happiness.
4. Power is *dravya*.
5. Quality is *tamas*.
6. By the identification with the deep-sleep state, the individual is known as *prājña*.

Q. 124: What is the example to understand deep-sleep state?

Ans: Example [1]. (1) It is like a person whose ornaments fall into a well, another goes down the well to fetch the ornaments. When that person gets the ornaments, it is known, and when the person does not get the ornament, it is also known. (2) The means to speak is the sense-organ of speech presided by Agni which is opposed to *jala* and hence is covered. Hence he does not speak. (3) When the person comes out of water then he obtains the sense-organ of speech along with [the blessing of] the presiding deity. The person now says whether he fetched the ornaments or not.

Explanation: In the same way, (1) There is a general knowledge of bliss and ignorance in the deep-sleep state because of the witness consciousness. (2) But, there [in deep-sleep state] the sense-organs and internal organ are absent [resolved] which are the means for specific knowledge. Therefore, there is no specific knowledge of happiness or ignorance. (3) When the person wakes up, the means for specific knowledge — sense-organs and internal organ — are available. Then, there is the recollection of the experience of bliss and ignorance in deep-sleep state in the form of specific knowledge.

Example [2]. Just as (1) the *ghee* is liquid when in contact with heat. (2) In shade, the *ghee* becomes hard. (3) Again, by contact with heat the *ghee* melts into liquid.

Explanation: Similarly (1) in deep sleep, there is the causal body in the form of ignorance. (2) In waking and dream states it is the intellect (*buddhi*). (3) Again, in deep sleep it is in the form of ignorance.

Example [3]. As (1) a child goes out to play with his friends. (2) When tired, he resorts to the lap of the mother and experiences the happiness at home. (3) Again, when the friends call the child, he goes out to play.

Explanation: In the same way, (1) the causal body which is ignorance is like the mother. The intellect (*buddhi*) is likened to the child of the nature of action that plays with his friends, likened to waking and dream states, in the playground, i.e. the transactions are carried out in the external world. (2) When tiredness in the form of *vikṣepa* is experienced, one comes back home likened to deep sleep into the lap of the mother compared to ignorance, where one resolves and experiences the bliss nature of *Brahman*. (3) Again, when the action likened to children's call, one plays in the external world of waking and dream states.

Example [4]. As (1) a pot is filled with water of the ocean (2) a rope is tied to its neck and merged in the ocean (3) then the water contained in the pot and the water of the ocean become one. (4) Then too, the pot which is an external factor is different (5). When the rope is drawn, the difference is known (6) but the pot with water and the ocean that has space as the substratum is non-different, (7) but it is one essence in the three periods of time.

Explanation: Similarly (1) ignorance comparable to water of the ocean, which is filled in the subtle body likened to the pot (2) being tied with the rope of *adr̥ṣṭa* it resolves during deep sleep or in death, swooning, dissolution into *Īśvara* whose adjunct is the *māyā* that is the total ignorance (3) the ignorance of the individual has the adjunct as *avidyā*. It merges into the macro ignorance (4) then also, the adjunct in the form of impressions in the subtle body is different (5) when the *adr̥ṣṭa* form rope is drawn inward the *antaryāmī* is invoked, the difference is known (6) but the micro ignorance likened to water within the subtle body likened to a pot, and the macro ignorance likened to ocean that has the space as its substratum, that is non-different (7) but the essence of the three periods is one.

Q. 125: From the deep-sleep state what gets established?

Ans: 1. The deep-sleep state is known to me.

2. The absence of waking and dream states is known to me.

I am not the deep-sleep state and it is not mine. It belongs to the causal body. I am the knower and witness of it as that of a pot. I am the witness of this third state namely the deep-sleep state.

Thus ends the fifth digit of *Vicāracandrodaya* titled "I Am the Witness of the Three States".

Kalā 6

Falsity of the World

ललित छंद (*Lalita* Metre)[83]

सकलदृश्य सो-ऽध्यास छोडना।
जगअधारमैं चित्त जोडना।।

त्रयदशाहि जो जाग्रदादि हैं।
सबप्रपंच सो भिन्न नाहिं हैं।। ६ ।।

रजत आदि हैं सीपिमैं यथा।
त्रयदशा सु हैं ब्रह्ममैं तथा।।

रजतआदिवत् दृश्य ये मृषा।
शुगतिकादिवत् ब्रह्म अमृषा।। ७ ।।

व्यभिचरैं मिथो रजतआदि ज्यों।
इनहिकी मिथो व्यावृती जु त्यों।।

शुगति सूत्रवत् अनुग एक जो।
अनुवृतीयुतो ब्रह्म आप सो।। ८ ।।

शुगतिकामहीं तीनअंश ज्यूं।
अजडब्रह्ममैं तीनअंश त्यूं।।

उभयअंशकूं सत्य जानिले।
त्रतिय त्यागदे मोक्ष तौ मिले।। ९ ।।

भिदभ्रमादि जो पंचधाभवं।
त्रिविधतापता तप्त सो दवं।

परशु पंचधा-युक्तियों करी।
करि विचार तूं छेद ना डरी।। १० ।।

---

83 It is similar to the metre of *Gopikāgīta* in the 10th *skandha*, chap. 31 of *Śrīmad Bhāgavata*.

नहि जु जाहिमैं तीनकालमैं।
तहँहि भान व्है मध्यकालमैं।।

शुगति रौप्यवत् ध्यास सो भ्रमं।
अरथ ज्ञान दो-भांतिका क्रमं।। ११ ।।

द्विविधवेम है ज्ञान अर्थको।
अरथभ्रांति वा षड्‌विधा बको।।

सकलध्यास जे जगतमैं दसे।
सबसु याहिके बीचमैं धसे।। १२ ।।

निज चिदात्मकूं ब्रह्म जानिके।
सकलवेमको मूल भानिके।।

परममोदकूं आप बूजिले।
इहहि मुक्ति पीतांबरो मिले।। १३ ।।

sakaladr̥śya so 'dhyāsa choḍanā।
jaga adhāramaiṅ citta joḍanā।।

trayadaśāhi jo jāgradādi haiṅ।
sabaprapañca so bhinna nāhiṅ haiṅ।। 6 ।।

rajata ādi haiṅ sīpimaiṅ yathā।
trayadaśā su haiṅ brahmamaiṅ tathā।।

rajataādivat dr̥śya ye mr̥ṣā।
śugatikādivat brahma amr̥ṣā।। 7 ।।

vyabhicaraiṅ mitho rajata ādi jyoṅ।
inahikī mitho vyāvr̥tī ju tyoṅ।।

śugati sūtravat anuga eka jo।
anuvr̥tīyuto brahma āpa so।। 8 ।।

śugatikāmahīṅ tīna aṁśa jyūṅ।
ajaḍabrahmaiṅ tīna aṁśa tyūṅ।।

ubhaya aṁśakūṁ satya jānile।
tratiya tyāgade mokṣa tau mile।। 9 ।।

bhidabhramādi jo pañcadhābhavaṁ |
trividhatāpatā tapta so davaṁ |
paraśu pañcadhā-yuktiyoṅ karī |
kari vicāra tūṅ cheda nā ḍarī || 10 ||

nahi ju jāhimaiṅ tīnakālamaiṅ |
tahaṁhi bhāna vhai madhyakālamaiṅ ||

śugati raupyavat dhyāsa so bhramaṁ |
aratha jñāna do-bhāṅtikā kramaṁ || 11 ||

dvividhavema hai jñāna arthako |
arathabhrānti vā ṣaḍvidhā bako ||

sakaladhyāsa je jagatamaiṅ dase |
sabasu yāhike bīcamaiṅ dhase || 12 ||

nija cidātmakūṁ brahma jānike |
sakalavemako mūla bhānike ||

paramamodakūṁ āpa būjile |
ihahi mukti pītāṁbaro mile || 13 ||

All that is perceptible is error so give up
fix mind in the substratum of the universe.

The three states[84] namely waking state,
and the entire universe are not different. || 6 ||

Just as silver is seen on a shell,
the three states are seen on *Brahman*.

The perceptible is false like silver etc.,
Brahman is truth[85] like shell etc. || 7 ||

Mutually[86] changing are silver etc.,[87]
and they are mutually different.[88]

---

84 Three states of experience.

85 Reality.

86 Mutual.

87 Etc. refers to mica and paper.

88 The kind of difference is mutual non-existence, *anyonyābhāva*.

Like shell there is one thread,[89]
inherent[90] which is you *Brahman* ॥ 8 ॥

As there are three parts[91] in the shell,
similarly there are three parts in non-inert *Brahman*
of which, two are to be known as real[92]
by giving up the third,[93] liberation is gained ॥ 9 ॥

[94]Difference, delusion, etc. constitute the five abode[95]
one is scorched in the thickness[96] by threefold miseries.

With fivefold reasoning [like] axe,[97]
undertake enquiry and uproot without fear ॥ 10 ॥

Not known in the three periods of times
but evident in between
[seeing] shell like coin is error which is delusion,
object[98] and knowledge are twofold delusion in this order ॥ 11 ॥

twofold delusions[99] — knowledge and its object,
[100]Object-delusion is known to be sixfold.

---

[89] Like the thread in a garland of flowers.

[90] Immanent.

[91] General, Specific and Specific-Imagined are the three parts.

[92] General and Specific — these two "parts".

[93] The third is the imagined part.

[94] Beginning from difference, delusion, etc. Here, etc. means the delusion of doership, enjoyership, delusion of relation, delusion of modification, delusion that world is real and different from *Brahman*. These four are to be known as delusions.

[95] Five types of bondage.

[96] [Dense] forest.

[97] To be read as: with five kinds of reasons compared to an axe. [See Q. 129.]

[98] Delusion here means error. Object refers to object-error (*arthādhyāsa*) and knowledge refers to knowledge-error (*jñānādhyāsa*). In this manner, there are twofold delusions.

[99] Knowledge means knowledge-error and object means object-error. Delusion here refers to error. Each of them is twofold.

[100] Object-delusion is object-error that is of six types.

All errors included[101] in the world,
gets conjoined in between[102] || 12 ||

Know oneself as *Brahman*,
by removing the root[103] of all errors
recognize the Absolute Happiness[104]
this liberation is gained by Pitambar || 13 ||

Q. 126: How do the three states illumine in Self?

Ans: Example: Like silver or mica or paper in a shell which is imagined on a shell due to ignorance, these three entities,

1. are mutually different from the shell and
2. these are same as the shell.

Like:

1. [1] When silver is seen in a shell, the mica and paper are not known and

   [2] when mica is seen, then silver and paper are not known and

   [3] when paper is seen, then silver and mica are not known. Thus the three entities are mutually different. In the beginning, middle and end of the shell, there is absolute non-existence of these three entities at the empirical and transcendental levels.

2. At the time of delusion

   [1] "this is silver"

   [2] "this is mica"

   [3] "this is paper"

in this way, the "this" part of the shell is immanently present in these three entities. The three entities are the same as the shell.

---

[101] Shown [seen].

[102] Obtains entry.

[103] Ignorance.

[104] Know the Absolute Happiness *Brahman* as Self.

There are three parts in the shell — (1) general part, (2) specific part, and (3) imagined specific part.

[1] The general part is "this" that which is known for more period of time is known as the general part. Just as the "this" is

1. known during the time of delusion and
2. in the absence of delusion also it is present when referred to as "this is shell".

Thus, "this" is the general part and is the substratum (*ādhāra*).

[2] The specific part is the blue colour, triangular shape of the shell. That which is known for a less period of time is known as specific part.

1. at the time of delusion, the blue colour etc. are not known
2. but by the knowledge of these features, the delusion is gone.

Thus, it is the specific part and is the support (*adhiṣṭhāna*).

[3] Silver etc. are the imagined specific parts. That which does not manifest at the time of the knowledge of the support is the imagined specific part. As

1. silver, etc. are seen when one is ignorant of the shell.
2. when the shell is known, silver does not manifest.
3. it is different from the shell.

Thus, it is the imagined specific part and is known as delusion (*bhrānti*).

Explanation: Just as in the substratum Self there is the delusion of waking, dream or deep-sleep states, these three delusions happen due to the ignorance of Self.

1. They are mutually different (*vyatireka*)[105] from the substratum Self.
2. Self is constant (*anvaya*).[106]

[1] 1. When waking state is experienced then the dream and deep-sleep states are not experienced.
2. When dream state is experienced then the waking and deep-sleep states are not experienced.
3. When deep-sleep state is experienced then the waking and dream states are not experienced.

These three states are mutually different. These three states are absolutely non-existent in the substratum at the transcendental level (always absent). These three states are different from the substratum. And

[2] Self is immanent and luminous in these three states. These states are the same as the Self.

Here due to adjunct of ignorance three parts are superimposed on Self. (1) General part, (2) specific part, and (3) imagined specific part.

[1] Existence (is-ness) is the general part. That is,

1. "waking state is", "dream state is", "deep-sleep state is", the Existence of Self is known during the time of delusion. And
2. at the removal of delusion "I am Existence", "I am Consciousness", "I am Absolute Peace", "I am Complete", "I am Unassociated", "I am Eternally Liberated", "I am *Brahman*", in this way the Existence of Self is revealed and this nature of Existence is the general part and it is the substratum.

---

105 Non-existence or obstruction is known as different.

106 Existent or unobstruction is known as constant.

[2] The "attributes" of Self are Consciousness, Absolute Peace, Unassociated, Non-dual, etc. These are the specific parts. As,

1. at the time of delusion these are not known but
2. by the knowledge of these attributes the delusion is removed.

Hence, these are specific parts and are the support.

[3] The three states of experiences are the imagined specific part. As,

1. *Brahman* that is non-different from *ātman* manifests during ignorance.
2. "I am *Brahman*" by gaining such knowledge of Self, Existence different from Self is not seen.

The superimposed three states are imagined specific parts and it is known as delusion.

In this way, these three states in Self are said to be false.

Q. 127: What are the other examples to show the superimposition of false world on Self?

Ans: They are

1. a person seen in the place of a tree.
2. a dream seen in the place of witness (consciousness).
3. mirage-water seen in desert land.
4. seeing blueness in sky.
5. seeing rope as snake.
6. seeing inverted trees or human in water.
7. seeing town in a mirror.

These are false. Similarly, due to ignorance the world is [seen] which is false, instead of [knowing the] Self. In this way, ascertaining the falsity of the world alone is known as sublation[107] of the world.

Q. 128: How many kinds of bondage in the form of delusion are there?

Ans: 1. Delusion of difference[108]

2. Delusion of doership and enjoyership[109]

3. Delusion of association[110]

4. Delusion of transformation[111]

5. Delusion of reality of world other than *Brahman.*

These are five types of bondage in the form of delusion.

Q. 129: How are these fivefold delusions removed? Explain with examples.

Ans: 1. The delusion of difference is resolved by the example of original–reflection.[112]

2. By the example of perception of red colour in a crystal

---

107 Sublation means ascertaining the falsity of the world. It is [known from] three sources — scriptures, logic and direct.

108 There are five kinds of "difference-delusion" [delusion in the form of difference] — (1) difference between *jīva* and *Īśvara,* (2) mutual difference in the *jīva*s, (3) mutual difference between inert entities, (4) difference between *jīva* and *jaḍa,* and (5) difference between *jaḍa* and *Īśvara.*

109 The attributes of the internal organ as doer, enjoyer are seen in Self. This sense of doership and enjoyership is delusion.

110 The sense of "I" with regard to the body, etc. and the sense of "mine" with regard to house, etc. are associated with Self. Or seeing the difference of homogeneity, heterogeneity and internal. This is called delusion of association.

111 Like the modification of milk into curd, considering the modification or transformation of *Brahman* into *jīva* and *jagat* is known as modification-based delusion.

112 Padmapādācārya's commentary to *Sūtra Bhāṣya* is known as *Pañcapādikā*. Prakāśātman's commentary to *Pañcapādikā* is *Vivaraṇa.* Here the example of original–reflection is discussed.

due to its proximity to a red cloth, the delusion of doership and enjoyership is removed.

3. By the example of pot–space, delusion of association is removed.
4. Delusion of modification is removed by the example of rope–snake.
5. The delusion of real world other than *Brahman* is removed by the example of gold and ear-ring (gold ornament).

Q. 130: How is the delusion of difference removed by the example of original–reflection?

Ans: As (1) the face gets reflected in the mirror and the reflection does not belong to the mirror but when the mirror is perceived, the mind through the eyes reaches the mirror and returns to the original face which is [actually] seen. Therefore, the original face as reflection in the mirror is non-different from the reflection. Thus, the reflection is not false, but real. (2) The features of reflection as different from the original, reflection seen in the mirror, and the features of reflection as opposite to the original — these three features and their knowledge is delusion. (3) These features are to be dismissed as false certainly and the non-difference between original and reflection is to be ascertained.

Explanation: As (1) *Brahman* is original. Ignorance is like mirror and *jīva* is the reflection. Like in dream, one *jīva* is real and various other animate and inanimate things are seen. This is semblance of *jīva*. The *jīva* reflection and original *Īśvara* are always non-different. But (2) due to the power of *māyā* the feature of *jīva* is seen as different from that of the original *Īśvara*. There is the notion of individuality, limited knowledge, limited power, limitation, plurality, etc., and the knowledge of these is delusion. (3) By dismissing these features as certainly false, the eternal non-difference between the reflection *jīva* and the original *Īśvara* is ascertained. In this way, by the example of original–reflection, the delusion of difference is removed.[113]

Q. 131: How is the delusion of doership and enjoyership uprooted by the example of red colour in crystal due to proximity to red cloth?

Ans: As (1) by the conjunction–association (*saṁyoga sambandha*) the red colour of the cloth is seen in the crystal (2) but it is the quality of the cloth (3). When the cloth and crystal are separated then the colour is not seen in the crystal (4) therefore, it is not the quality of the crystal (5) but it is seen due to delusion.

Explanation: As (1) the attributes of the internal organ are doership and enjoyership that is seen in Self due to the relation of identity (*tādātmya sambandha*) (2) but these are the qualities of the internal organ (3). During deep sleep, the mind and Self are "separated" wherein these features are not known (4) thus these are not the features of Self (5) but is seen in Self due to delusion.

In this way, by the example of red colour in crystal due to proximity to red cloth, the delusion of doership and enjoyership is uprooted.

Q. 132: How is the delusion of association eliminated by the example of pot–space?

Ans: As (1) the space confined within the adjunct pot is called pot–space (2) that space is associated with pot (3). The features of the pot are origination, destruction, appearing and disappearing but these do not affect the space (4) since space is unassociated. (5) The association of space is seen from the standpoint of pot which is a delusion.

---

[113] By the negation of the primary difference between *jīva* and *Īśvara*, the other four differences [refer footnote 108] get negated naturally. The difference is caused due to the adjunct. The adjunct is false and thus the difference caused by the adjunct is also false. Really, the non-dual *Brahman* alone remains.

Explanation: (1) Self in the limiting factor in the form of body etc. is the *jīva*. (2) The Self is illumined in association with the components. (3) The features of the components (body, mind, etc.) are subject to origination and destruction, and these features do not affect the Self. (4) Thus, Self is not associated with these components. (5) Self is not of the form of the component. Self is not the notion of "I" caused in the component and hence Self is not the component. But the components are the five elements. There is neither the notion of mine in Self which belongs to the component. Thus, Self is different from the components. There is no notion of "mine" in relation of the component in Self to wife, son, house, etc. Self is unassociated. The notion of "I" and "mine" with regard to component superimposed on Self is a delusion. In this way, by the example of pot–space the delusion of association is eliminated.

Q. 133: How does the rope–snake example destroy the delusion of transformation?

Ans: As (1) in a dim light there is a rope. The mind through the sense-organ of eye reaches the place of the rope, as in perceptual cognition. That thought, due to defects like darkness etc. does not obtain the form [of rope]. Therefore, by this thought the concealment of rope is not destroyed. The *tūla-avidyā*[114] in the Consciousness conditioned by rope is disturbed that transforms into snake [here]. (2) That "snake" is the modification of ignorance like the modification of milk into curd and (3) Consciousness conditioned by the rope is changeless. It does not modify (transform).

Explanation: As (1) the *mūla-avidyā*[115] rests on *Brahman*

---

114 *Tūla-avidyā* is that which conceals the Consciousness conditioned by pot etc.

115 The ignorance that conceals Pure *Brahman* and *ātman* is called *mūl-avidyā*.

Consciousness. By the disturbance (*kṣobha*)[116] of *prārabdha karma* there is the modification in the form of inert, consciousness (reflection) and world. (2) This world is a modification[117] of ignorance. (3) The substratum[118] which is *Brahman* Consciousness is subject to transfiguration[119] and not transformation. In this way, by the example of rope–snake the delusion of modification is destroyed.

Q. 134: How is the delusion of reality of world different from *Brahman* removed by the example of gold ornament?

Ans: As (1) the difference seen between gold and [gold] ear-ring as cause and effect is a delusion. (2) The [gold] ear-ring of a different nature other than the gold is not seen. (3) In reality, they are non-different. (4) Moreover, other than gold, the ear-ring does not have an existence of its own.

Explanation: As (1) the notion of cause–effect between *Brahman* and the world and the attribute of difference is imagined (2)

---

[116] The circumstance for action is called disturbance [here].

[117] (1) giving up the earlier form and assuming another form is called transformation.

(2) Or the modification into another, in the same order of reality as that of the material cause; the material cause and the change of the attribute are known as transformation. Just as transformation of milk is curd, this is also known as change [*upādāna-sama-sattāka-kāryāpattiḥ*].

[118] Substratum is that which remains free from modifications and is the support of superimpositions caused by ignorance. Just as the rope is the support of imagined snake, this is referred to as transfigurative material cause different from the transformative material cause [*upādāna-viṣama-sattāka-kāryāpattiḥ*].

[119] That which is of a different order of reality from that of the substratum, say is lower, which assumes a different name and attribute than that of the substratum is known as transfiguration. Just as the transfiguration of rope is snake, this is also known as imagined effect or imagined content.

on enquiry, the world of name (*nāma*) and form (*rūpa*) which is different from existence (*asti*), illumination (*bhāti*) and happiness (*priyam*) cannot be established as real. But it can be affirmed as false. A thing which is superimposed on an entity can never be different from that entity (3) really, there is non-difference between *Brahman* and the world. (4) Moreover, other than *Brahman*, the world does not have a separate existence of its own.

Q. 135: What is delusion?

Ans: Error is known as delusion.

Q. 136: What is error?

Ans: The false object which is the content of deluded knowledge and the deluded knowledge is known as error.

Q. 137: How many kinds of errors are there?

Ans: Error is of two kinds — knowledge-error (*jñānādhyāsa*) and object-error (*arthādhyāsa*). The object-error is [further classified as] the error due to relation only (*kevala-sambandha-adhyāsa*);[120] with relation inclusive of the error of relater (*sambandha-sahita-sambandhī adhyāsa*);[121] error of only the property (*kevala-dharma-adhyāsa*);[122] error of property and substance (*dharma-sahita-dharmī-adhyāsa*);[123] mutual error

120 When the features of non-self are superimposed on Self due to the relation of identity, and these attributes are not that of Self, this error of attribution of non-self on Self is known as error due to relation alone.

121 The superimposition of the relation and nature of the non-self on Self where along with relation of nonself on Self there is the error of relator [*sambandhī*] are known as error of relator.

122 The features of gross body like fairness etc. and the features of subtle body like sense of sight etc. are superimposed on self and not the nature of the three [bodies], this error of only the features of body and sense-organs on Self is error of attributes only.

123 The attributes of internal organ like doership, with its nature is superimposed on Self. Thus there is an error of attributes of

→

(*anyonya adhyāsa*);[124] error of any one (*anyatara adhyāsa*),[125] in this way there are six kinds of error.

Or, error of substance or nature (*svarūpādhyāsa*)[126] and error by association or relation (*saṁsargādhyāsa*)[127] are the two types of error.

1. the above-mentioned six types are included[128] and
2. They also include[129] the five kinds of delusion of difference mentioned earlier [see Q. 128].

→ internal organ with the substance and this is known as error of attribute and substance.

124 Like the iron and fire, the features of Self and non-self are mutually superimposed; this is known as mutual error.

125 Here, the nature of non-self is not superimposed on Self but the nature of Self is superimposed on non-self and this is known as error of any one. Of the two, this kind of error is the error of one on another.

126 That which is subject to negation by knowledge is superimposed on the nature of substratum. By the knowledge of the substratum the non-self like body etc. gets negated. This is known as error of the nature with regard to Self.

127 An entity which is never subject to negation will never undergo the error of nature (substance) but by its relation there arises an error. There is error by association of non-self with Self. This is known as error by relation or association.

128 Error only of the attribute, error caused by attribute with substance and error of any one — these three are included in the error of substance or nature. The error of only relation is the same as error of relation.

The error of relation with the relator is the error of association along with error of nature. In the mutual error, there is both error of relation and error of nature. (1) The nature of Self is real. There is no error but due to relation or relation of identity there is the superimposition of non-self, this is known as error of relation. (2) The nature of non-self is superimposed on Self and this is known as error of nature. Thus the mutual error [error of substance and error of association] is included in both.

129 The five kinds of delusion as delusion of difference etc., was →

1. the attributes of Self and non-self which give rise to mutual error, that are said later [see Q. 140], are also inclusive. These will be demonstrated in the footnotes [see footnotes 120 to 128].

Q. 138: What is specifically instrumental in knowing the superimposition of non-self as individuality, etc. and error of Self, i.e. of all kinds of error which kind of error is inherent in everything?

Ans: The mutual error.

Q. 139: What is mutual error?

Ans: The error of mutually transferring the features of one on to another is known as mutual error.[130]

Q. 140: In what manner, does the mutual error of Self and non-self take place?

Ans: [1-4] The four "features" of Self are Existence, Consciousness, Absolute Peace and Non-duality.

[1-4] The four features of non-self are non-existence, inert, sorrow and duality.

→ given earlier [Q. 128]. Of these, excluding the delusion of association the other four kinds of delusions are included in error of nature. The fifth kind of delusion, namely, delusion of association is included in error of association.

130 Here, the nature of each error is not explained elaborately with relevant examples due to problem of it becoming lengthy, but is given briefly. But the nature of mutual error and the specific instrument to know is given clearly. (1) The nature of non-self is sorrow with duality which is superimposed on the infinite and non-dual nature of Self that gets concealed. (2) The nature of Self is Existence and Consciousness, due to association they are superimposed on the non-existent and inert non-self which gets concealed. That which is concealed by ignorance along with its effects is the substratum. In this way, the mutual error of Self and non-self is also included in error of association and error of nature.

Of which,

[1-2] the sorrow and duality features of non-self conceal the absolute peace and non-dual nature of Self. Therefore only,

1. it is not known that "I am of the nature of absolute peace and non-dual"
2. but, is thought as "I am sorrowful and am different from *Īśvara*".

[3-4] The Existence and Consciousness nature of Self conceals the non-existence and inert nature of non-self and therefore the non-self assumes individuality,

1. "this is non-existent", "this is inert" — is not known.
2. but "it exists and is sentient" — is experienced.

In this way, there is mutual error[131] of Self and non-self.

Thus ends the sixth digit of *Vicāracandrodaya* titled "Falsity of the World".

---

[131] The mutual error of *Brahman* and *Īśvara,* and *kūṭastha* and *jīva* is discussed in the eleventh digit (chapter titled "Establishment of Oneness of the Word-meanings of Tat and Tvam") [see Qs. 207 and 210].

Kalā 7

Features of Self

इन्द्रविजय छंद (*Indravijaya* Metre[132])

आत्म विशेषण हैं जु दुभांति।
विधेय निषेध्य कहों निरधारे।।

वे सब जानि भले गुरु शास्त्र सु।
सो अपनो निजरूप निहारे।।

सच्चिदनंद रु ब्रह्म स्वयंपर-
काश कुटस्थ रु साक्षि विचारे।।

द्रष्ट्र अरु उपद्रष्ट्र रु एकहि।
आदि विधेय विशेषण धारे।। १४ ।।

अंतविहीन अखंड असंग रु।
अद्वय जन्मविना अविकारे।।

चारि अकारविना अरु व्यक्त।
न माननको विषयो जु निकारे।।

कर्म करीहि बढै न घटै इस।
हेतुहि अव्यय वेद पुकारे।।

अक्षर नाशविना कहिये इस।
आदि निषेध्य पीतांबर सारे।। १५ ।।

ātma viśeṣaṇa haiṅ ju dubhāṅti
vidheya niṣedhya kahoṅ niradhāre

ve saba jāni bhale guru śāstra su
so apano nijarūpa nihāre

saccidananda ru brahma svayaṁpara-
kāśa kuṭastha ru sākṣi vicāre

---

132 *Indravijaya* is sung in *ṭhumurī* and *lāvaṇī*.

draṣṭṭa aru upadraṣṭṭa ru ekahi ।
ādi vidheya viśeṣaṇa dhāre ।। 14 ।।

aṅtavihīna akhaṇḍa asaṅga ru ।
advaya janmavinā avikāre ।।

cāri akāravinā aru vyakta ।
na mānanako viṣayo ju nikāre ।।

karma karīhi baḍhai na ghaṭai isa ।
hetuhi avyaya veda pukāre ।।

akṣara nāśavinā kahiye isa ।
ādi niṣedhya pītāṁbara sāre ।। 15 ।।

There are two types of attributes,
primary and negatable attributes.

They[133] are known from *guru* and scriptures,
which reveal one's own nature.

Existence, Consciousness, Absolute Happiness and Self evident *Brahman*; *Kūṭastha* and *Sākṣī* are enquired into.

The seer and onlooker are one,
The beginning assumes primary attributes ।। 14 ।।

Without end,[134] indivisible and relationless,
non-dual, without birth,[135] free from modifications.

Without fourfold forms[136] and visible,
not as the object of means of knowledge[137]
by action, It does not grow nor perish
the cause is unchanging declares the Veda
imperishable, free from destruction is This
Pitambar, negates all the attributes ।। 15 ।।

---

133 Both the primary and negatable attributes.

134 Infinite.

135 Birthless.

136 Formless.

137 *Aprameya* [not an object of knowledge].

Q. 141: How many kinds of "features" are there for Self? [See also Q. 185.]

Ans: The features of Self are of two kinds — primary (*vidheya*)[138] which is directly cognized and negatable (*niṣedhya*)[139] which is known by the negation of the world.

Q. 142: What are the *vidheya* aspects of Self?

Ans: (1) Existence, (2) Consciousness, (3) Absolute Happiness, (4) Infinite, (5) Self-luminous, (6) Unchanging (*kūṭastha*), (7) Witness, (8) Seer, (9) Onlooker, (supervisor), (10) One, etc.

Q. 143: What is the Existence principle of Self?

Ans: (1) That which is known and that which is not negatable by anyone is Existence. Self is known and is not negatable by anyone and thus Self is Existence.

Q. 144: What is the Consciousness principle of Self?

Ans: (2) The unchanging light is Consciousness. Self is of unchanging light and thus Self is Consciousness.

Q. 145: What is the Absolute Happiness principle of Self?

Ans: (3) It is said to be the most supreme and is the content of highest love that is Absolute Happiness. Self is greatly loved by all and hence Self is of the nature of Absolute Happiness.

Q. 146: What is the Infinite nature of Self?

Ans: (4) (1) Self is Existence, Consciousness and Absolute Happiness in nature and is validated by scripture, logic and experience.

---

138 Just as the word *sadhavā* (a woman whose husband is alive). This word negates a widow and results in the direct knowledge of her non-widow state. Likewise, the word "Existence" negates the world as non-existent and results in the direct knowledge of *Brahman* as existence. Hence it is called *vidheya*.

139 Just as the word *avidhavā* negates a widow, i.e. it indicates a non-widow who is different from a widow, words like "infinite" are "negative attributes" that negate the world as finite and reveal the infinite *Brahman* which is different from the finite world. This is called as *niṣedhya*.

(2) Infinite (*Brahman*) is the subject matter of scripture (Upaniṣads) which is known as Existence, Consciousness and Absolute Happiness. Thus, Self is of the nature of *Brahman*. The name *Brahman* means all-pervasive. That which is not limited in space is known as all-pervasive.

1. If Self is different from *Brahman* then it is said to be limited by space.
2. That which is limited by space is limited by time also. This is the maxim.

That which is limited by space and time is non-eternal. Then Self will be non-eternal.

Thus, Self is not different from *Brahman*.

1. If *Brahman* is said to be different from Self then *Brahman* will be non-self.
2. The non-self like pot is inert. Then *Brahman* different from Self will be inert.

This contradicts the statement of the scripture. Thus, *Brahman* is not different from Self, i.e. Self is of the nature of *Brahman*.

Q. 147: What is the Self-luminous principle of Self?

Ans: (5) (1) That which like a lamp does not depend on another for its illumination and (2) that which illumines everything, is known as Self-luminous. The Self is of this nature. Thus, Self is Self-luminous.

Or,

1. that which is always direct and
2. is never an object of knowledge

is Self-luminous.

Self is always direct and being of the nature of light is never an object of knowledge [being known]. Thus, Self is Self-luminous.

Q. 148: What is the Unchanging principle (*kūṭastha*) of Self?

Ans: (6) *Kūṭa* is the anvil used by a blacksmith. Like that, which is unchanging and firm is known as *kūṭastha*. Just as the blacksmith, hammers the iron piece on the anvil, but it remains as it is, in the same way, the iron-like mind undergoes various hammering-like activities but the Self remains as it is. Thus, Self is *kūṭastha*. This word indicates immovable and non-action also.

Q. 149: What is the Witness principle of Self?

Ans: (7) (1) In the worldly transaction,

[1] that which remains indifferent, free from likes and dislikes

[2] that which is proximate and

[3] that which is sentient

is the nature of Witness principle. Self

[1] is indifferent to body etc.

[2] is proximate

[3] is sentient that illumines the insentient entities.

Thus, Self is the Witness principle.

(2) Or, the sentient principle in the internal organ adjunct is called the Witness principle.

(3) Or, mere Consciousness principle present in mind and in thought-modification of mind is the Witness principle. Self is of this nature and hence Self is the Witness principle.

Q. 150: What is the Seer nature of Self?

Ans: (8) Seer is one who sees. Self is the knower of everything seen. So Self is the Seer.

Q. 151: What is the Onlooker nature of Self?

Ans: (9) Just as,

[15] in a sacrificial ground, the activity of ritual is supervised by fifteen priests

[16] the sixteenth is the ritualist

[17] the seventeenth is the ritualist's wife

[18] the eighteenth is the onlooker who sits close-by and sees the entire activity without doing any action,

in the same manner,

[1-15] in the sacrificial ground like the gross body the five sense-organs of knowledge, the five sense-organs of action and the five vital airs are like the fifteen priests.

[16] the sixteenth is mind like the ritualist

[17] the seventeenth is the intellect like the ritualist's wife

[18] each of the above involves in their respective fields and engage in activities and reap the results and in proximate to all these is the Self of the nature of knowledge which is the eighteenth principle, the Onlooker.

Q. 152: How is the Self "One"?

Ans: (10) Since there is no [another] homogeneous Self it is said to be One. These are the *vidheya* features of Self.

Q. 153: What are the Negating (*niṣedhya*) features of Self?

Ans: (1) Limitless (*ananta*), (2) Indivisible, (3) Unassociated, (4) Non-dual, (5) Birthless, (6) Unmodifying, (7) Formless, (8) Unmanifest, (9) Undecaying, (10) Imperishable, etc.

Q. 154: What is the Limitless nature of Self?

Ans: [1]
1. Self is all-pervasive. It is not bound by space.
2. Self is eternal. It is not bound by time.
3. Self being the substratum of everything is the nature of all. It is not bound by another entity.

Thus, Self is not limited by space, time or another entity and hence it is Limitless.

Q. 155: What is the Indivisible nature of Self?

Ans: [2]
1. *Jīva* is different from *Īśvara*. *Jīva*s are mutually different. *Jīva* and inert world are different. Inert world is different from *Īśvara*. Inert and inert

entities are different. These are five differences and Self is free from these differences. Or,

2. Self is free from differences in the form of homogeneous, heterogeneous and internal divisions.

So, Self is indivisible.

Q. 156: How is Self said to be Unassociated?

Ans: [3] Association means relation. Relation is of three kinds (1) Relation within homogeneous entities, (2) relation between heterogeneous entities, and (3) relation within the internal divisions.

(1) Relation with one's own class is known as homogeneous relation. Like a brāhmaṇa associating with another brāhmaṇa.

(2) Relation with one of other class is known as heterogeneous relation. Like a brāhmaṇa associating with a śūdra.

(3) The relation of various limbs of the body is known as internal relation. Just as a brāhmaṇa is related with his own hand, leg, head and other limbs.

(1). [1] Self is (sentient) One. So, it does not have a class. And

[2] the differences like *jīva, Īśvara,* Brahmā, Viṣṇu and Śiva are caused by the adjuncts and therefore they are false.

Then, with what will Self have homogeneous relation?

(2). Self is Non-dual and Existent principle. The *māyā* (ignorance) and its effects in the form of gross and subtle universes that are perceived are not existent, there is no entity.

Then, with what will Self have heterogeneous relation?

(3). Self is partless and the aspects like Existence, Consciousness and Absolute Happiness are not parts of Self. Self being One, how will it have internal relation?

In this way, Self is free from all kinds of relations. Hence it is unassociated.

Q. 157: How is it a Non-dual Self?

Ans: [4] Duality of world is like the dream-world imagined which is not real. Self is free from duality and it is non-dual.

Q. 158: How is it a Birthless Self? [See also Q. 57.]

Ans: [5] The quality of gross body is origination. This quality [of origination] is not even in the subtle body then how can it be the attribute of the Self?

Moreover, if the birth of Self is accepted then death of Self is to be accepted. Then, Self will be non-eternal. The Orthodox School that holds on to the idea of another world does not favour this view. It is said,

1. that which is subject to birth and death has absence of beginning and end. That is, there is no Self in the past birth and it does not have any *karma*. Then, in this birth, without *karma*, the Self is subject to experiences and
2. after death Self does not remain, by this the *karma* done in this birth gets destroyed without being experienced.

Thus, the *karma* prescribed in the Veda will be redundant. So, the nature of Self is not subject to birth. Thus, Self is birthless. Birthless also means ageless, immortal.

Q. 159: How is Self said to be Unmodifying?

Ans: [6] (1) Origin of pot, (2) manifestation of its existence, (3) growth, (4) modification, (5) decay, and (6) destruction are the six properties of pot, but not of the space within the pot. Similarly,

1. "body is born" — this is birth
2. "body emerges" — this is existence (earlier it was not, now it is)
3. "body becomes a boy" — this is growth

4. "body is youth" — this is modification
5. "body is old" — this is decaying
6. "body is dead" — this is destruction.

These six modifications are the properties of the body and not of the knower of the body that is different from the body.

In this way, Self being free from six modifications is unmodifying.

Q. 160: What is meant by Formless Self?

Ans: [7] (1) Gross, (2) subtle, (3) long, and (4) short. These four kinds are the forms found in the world.

(1) Self being the non-object of sense-organ and mind is subtle and hence not gross.

(2) Self is all-pervasive, it is neither subtle nor atomic (small).

(3-4) Self is both the warp and woof of everything and hence is neither long nor short. Self is formless.

Q. 161: What is the Unmanifest nature of Self?

Ans: [8] Self is imperceptible by sense-organ and mind, and hence is said to be indescribable, i.e. Self is of Unmanifest nature.

Q. 162: How is Self said to be "Partless"?

Ans: [9] Just as the grains in a basket can be separated into parts, Self cannot be separated. Self is Partless.

Q. 163: How is Self said to be Imperishable?

Ans: [10] If Self is perishable it is subject to destruction. Self is imperishable. It is also known as *akṣaya*, immortal, indestructible.

These are the *niṣedhya* features of Self.

Q. 164: If these are said to be the "features" of Self how can it be said that they are mutually non-different?

Ans: The principles like Existence, Consciousness and Absolute Happiness are mutually non-different. These are not the qualities of Self but is its very nature. Hence they are not mutually different, but non-different.

1. The One Self is free from destruction. So it is said as Existence.
2. Different from inert object it is of the nature of light (*prakāśa*). So it is said as Consciousness.
3. Contrary to grief is (Self which is) the object of supreme love, so it is said as Absolute Happiness.

In this way, all the other features are to be known.

Example —

Just as one person from

1. the standpoint of father is the son
2. the standpoint of grandfather is the grandson
3. the standpoint of brother is the brother
4. the standpoint of uncle is the nephew.

Or, just as one mendicant

1. from the standpoint of animals, householder, *adaṇḍī*, etc. is seen as a human who has renounced and taken the stick (mendicant's staff). This is the *vidheya* kind of attribute.
2. from the standpoint of pot, stone, tree, etc., is the negating feature like non-pot, non-stone and non-tree.

In this way there is no mutual difference in the features of Self but they are non-different.

Thus ends the seventh digit of *Vicāracandrodaya* titled "Features of Self".

Kalā 8

Existence, Consciousness, Absolute Happiness

इन्द्रविजय छंद (*Indravijaya* Metre)

सच्चिदनंदसरूपहि मैं यह।
सद्गुरुके मुखसैं पहिचान्यो।।

जागृत स्वप्न सुषुप्ति जु आदिक।
तीनहुँ कालहिमैं परमान्यो।।

जागृतआदि लयाविध तीनहुं।
कालहि हों इसतैं सत मान्यो।।

तीनहुँ कालविषै सब जानहुँ।
या हित मैं चिदरूपहि जान्यो।। १६ ।।

मैं प्रिय हुं धन पुत्र रु पुद्गल-
आदिकतैं त्रयकाल अगान्यो।।

आतमअर्थ सबे प्रिय आतम।
आपहि है प्रिय दुःख नसान्यो।।

या हित मैं सबतैं प्रियतम्म रु।
हों परमानंद दुःखहि भान्यो।।

देह दशादि अतीत सु आतम।
पूरणब्रह्म पीतांबर गान्यो।। १७ ।।

saccidanandasarūpahi maiṅ yaha।
sadguruke mukhasaiṅ pahicānyo।।

jāgr̥ta svapna suṣupti ju ādika।
tīnahum̐ kālahimaiṅ paramānyo।।

jāgr̥ta ādi layāvidha tīnahuṁ।
kālahi hoṅ isataiṅ sata mānyo।।

tīnahuṁ kālaviṣai saba jānahuṁ ।
yā hita maiṅ cidarūpahi jānyo ।। 16 ।।

maiṅ priya huṁ dhana putra ru pudgala-
ādikataiṅ trayakāla agānyo ।।

ātama artha sabe priya ātama ।
āpahi hai priya duḥkha nasānyo ।।

yā hita maiṅ sabataiṅ priyatamma ru ।
hoṅ paramānanda duḥkhahi bhānyo ।।

deha daśādi atīta su ātama ।
pūraṇabrahma pītāṁbara gānyo ।। 17 ।।

I am of the nature of Existence, Consciousness, Absolute Happiness,
know from the teachings of a *guru*.

Waking, dream and deep sleep states,
these three are within time and I am different from these.

Waking etc., up to resolution, these three
are indeed time, know the Existence within
the experience of the three states that are known,
know this awareness as Consciousness ।। 16 ।।

I am loved — wealth, son and body[140] —
etc., in three periods of time is not complete.[141]

Everything is loved for the sake of oneself
liked when favourable and otherwise is sorrow.

Of the favoured the most loved one
is the absolute happiness devoid of sorrow.

Self is beyond body, space,[142] etc.,
Infinite *Brahman* Pītambar is complete ।। 17 ।।

---

140 Physical body.

141 There is no contentment.

142 The three states of experience.

Q. 165: What is Existence?

Ans: (1) That which remains unsublated [not negated] in three periods of time is Existence.

Q. 166: What is Consciousness?

Ans: (2) That which knows everything in three periods of time is Consciousness.

Q. 167: What is Absolute Happiness?

Ans: (3) That which is the object of supreme love in three periods of time is Absolute Happiness.

Q. 168: "I am Existence". How to know this?

Ans: (1) I am the content of the three periods of time. So I am Existence. This is to be known.

Q. 169: "I am the content of the three periods of time". How to know this?

Ans: [1] 1. I am the content of waking state
2. I am the content of dream state
3. I am the content of deep-sleep state

[2] 1. I am the content of morning
2. I am the content of afternoon
3. I am the content of evening

[3] 1. I am the content of day
2. I am the content of night
3. I am the content of fortnight

[4] 1. I am the content of months
2. I am the content of seasons
3. I am the content of rain

[5] 1. I am the content of the childhood
2. I am the content of youth state
3. I am the content of old age

[6] 1. I am the content of earlier body(*)
2. I am the content of the current body
3. I am the content of future body

(*Present tense is used here while referring to the past and future. It indicates the falsity of past etc. Self as Existence, etc. is declared by the Śruti and there is no means of knowledge to prove the non-existence of Self. By this it is proved that Self is Existence, Consciousness, Absolute Happiness at all times. This is to be known.)

Q. 170: How to know name, form and entities along with three periods of time as different from Me?

Ans: The name, form and entities along with three periods of time that are different from Me are to be known as non-existent.

Q. 171: By what is existence and non-existence ascertained?

Ans: By the logic of co-presence and co-absence (*anvaya-vyatireka*) the existence and non-existence can be ascertained.

Q. 172: How to ascertain existence and non-existence through the logic of co-presence (co-p) and co-absence (co-a)?

Ans: (1)

(co-p) I am the content [witness] of waking state
I am the content of dream state
Therefore I am Existence

(co-a) Waking state is not my content
This waking state is non-existent

(co-p) I am the content of dream state
I am the content of deep-sleep state
Therefore I am Existence

(co-a) Dream state is not my content
This dream state is non-existent

(co-p) I am the content of deep-sleep state
I am the content of morning
Therefore I am Existence

(co-a) Deep-sleep state is not Me
This deep sleep is non-existent

(2)

(co-p) I am the content of morning
I am the content of afternoon
Therefore I am Existence

(co-a) Morning is not Me
This morning is non-existent

(co-p) I am the content of afternoon
I am the content of evening
Therefore I am Existence

(co-a) Afternoon is not Me
This afternoon is non-existent

(co-p) I am the content of evening
I am the content of day
Therefore I am Existence

(co-a) Evening is not Me
This evening is non-existent

(3)

(co-p) I am the content of day
I am the content of night
Therefore I am Existence

(co-a) Day is not Me
This day is non-existent

(co-p) I am the content of night
I am the content of fortnight
Therefore I am Existence

(co-a) Night is not Me
This night is non-existent

(co-p) I am the content of fortnight
I am the content of month
Therefore I am Existence

(co-a) Fortnight is not Me
This fortnight is non-existent

(4)

(co-p) I am the content of month
I am the content of season
Therefore I am Existence

(co-a) Month is not Me
This month is non-existent

(co-p) I am the content of season
I am the content of rain
Therefore I am Existence

(co-a) Season is not Me
This season is non-existent

(co-p) I am the content of rain
I am the content of childhood
Therefore I am Existence

(co-a) Rain is not Me
This rain is non-existent

(5)

(co-p) I am the content of childhood
I am the content of youth
Therefore I am Existence

(co-a) Childhood is not Me
This childhood is non-existent

(co-p) I am the content of youth
I am the content of old age
Therefore I am Existence

(co-a) Youth is not Me
This youth is non-existent

(co-p) I am the content of old age
I am the content of previous body
Therefore I am Existence

(co-a) Old age is not Me
This old age is non-existent

(6)

(co-p) I am the content of previous body
I am the content of present body

Therefore I am Existence
(co-a) Previous body is not Me
The previous body is non-existent
(co-p) I am the content of the present body
I am the content of future body
Therefore I am Existence
(co-a) Present body is not Me
This present body is non-existent
(co-p) I am the content of future body
I am the content of *yuga*
Therefore I am Existence
(co-a) Future body is not Me
The future body is non-existent

(7)
(co-p) I am the content of *yuga*
I am the content of Manu
Therefore I am Existence
(co-a) *Yuga* is not Me
This *yuga* is non-existent
(co-p) I am the content of Manu
I am the content of *kalpa*
Therefore I am Existence
(co-a) Manu is not Me
Manu is non-existent
(co-p) I am the content of *kalpa*
I am the content of past period
Therefore I am Existence
(co-a) *Kalpa* is not Me
This *kalpa* is non-existent

(8)
(co-p) I am the content of past period
I am the content of future period
Therefore I am Existence
(co-a) Past period is not Me
Past period is non-existent

(co-p) I am the content of future period
I am the content of present time
Therefore I am Existence

(co-a) Future period is not Me
The future period is non-existent

(co-p) I am the content of present time
I am the content of all times
Therefore I am Existence

(co-a) Present time is not Me
Present time is non-existent.

In this way the existence and non-existence are to be determined by the reasoning of co-presence and co-absence.

Q. 173: How is that "I am Consciousness"?

Ans: (2) I know the experience in three periods of time. Therefore I am Consciousness.

Q. 174: "I know the experience in three periods of time therefore I am Consciousness" — How to know this?

Ans: (1) [1] I know the waking state
[2] I know the dream state
[3] I know the deep-sleep state

(2) [1] I know the morning
[2] I know the afternoon
[3] I know the evening

(3) [1] I know the day
[2] I know the night
[3] I know the fortnight

(4) [1] I know the month
[2] I know the season
[3] I know the rain

(5) [1] I know the childhood

[2] I know the youth

[3] I know the old age

(6) [1] I know the previous body

[2] I know the present body

[3] I know the future body

(7) [1] I know the *yuga*

[2] I know the Manu

[3] I know the *kalpa*

(8) [1] I know the past period

[2] I know the future period

[3] I know the present period

In this way I know all the periods. Therefore "I am Consciousness" is to be known.

Q. 175: How to know name, form and entity along with time as different from Me?

Ans: The name, form and entity along with time that are different from Me are to be known as inert.

Q. 176: How to ascertain Consciousness and inert entity?

Ans: By the logic of co-presence and co-absence the Consciousness and Matter can be ascertained.

Q. 177: How is the logic of co-presence and co-absence established to ascertain Consciousness and inert entity?

Ans: (1)

(Co-p) I know the waking state
I know the dream state
Therefore I am Consciousness

(Co-a) Waking state does not know Me
So, waking state is inert

(Co-p) I know the dream state
I know the deep-sleep state

Therefore I am Consciousness

(Co-a) Dream state does not know Me

So, dream state is inert.

In this way, the Consciousness and Matter are to be determined by applying the logic of co-presence and co-absence.

Q. 178: How is that "I am Absolute Happiness"?

Ans: (3) I am the content of Supreme Love in three periods of time. Therefore I am Absolute Happiness.

Q. 179: How to know that I am the (object) of Supreme Love in three periods of time?

Ans: [1] (1) I am the object of love in waking state

(2) I am the object of love in dream state

(3) I am the object of love in deep-sleep state

[2] (1) I am the object of love in morning

(2) I am the object of love in afternoon

(3) I am the object of love in evening

[3] (1) I am the object of love in day

(2) I am the object of love in night

(3) I am the object of love in fortnight

[4] (1) I am the object of love in month

(2) I am the object of love in season

(3) I am the object of love in rain

[5] (1) I am the object of love in childhood

(2) I am the object of love in youth

(3) I am the object of love in old age

[6] (1) I am the object of love in previous body

(2) I am the object of love in present body

(3) I am the object of love in future body

[7] (1) I am the object of love in *yuga*

(2) I am the object of love in Manu

(3) I am the object of love in *kalpa*

[8] (1) I am the object of love in past period

(2) I am the object of love in future period

(3) I am the object of love in present period

In this way I am the object of love in three periods of time. Therefore "I am Absolute Happiness" is to be known.

Q. 180: How to know name, form and entity along with time as different from Me?

Ans: The name, form, entity along with time that is other than Me is to be known as bondage (sorrow).

Q. 181: How to ascertain happiness and sorrow?

Ans: Happiness and sorrow can be ascertained by the logic of co-presence and co-absence.

Q. 182: How to establish the logic of co-presence and co-absence to ascertain happiness and sorrow?

Ans:

(Co-p) I am the object of (Supreme) Love in waking state
I am the object of love in dream state
Therefore I am Absolute Happiness.[143]

(Co-a) The waking state is not the object of love for Me
Therefore the waking state is sorrow

In this way the happiness and sorrow are to be ascertained by the logic of co-presence and co-absence.

143 The states like waking are known due to *ātmā*. When there is the experience of sorrow then also,

[1] the love of Self illumines through the reflected consciousness which is erroneously known to be happiness belonging to the waking state. This happiness does not illumine in other states of experience. There is thus an experience of love that varies in different times. This is really sorrow.

[2] There is always non-varying love with respect to Self. So, Self is of the nature of *ānanda*.

Q. 183: "I am the object of Supreme Love" — How to know this?

Ans: 1. The son's friend is loved for the sake of son.

2. Son is loved but not for the sake of friend.

So, son is loved more.

1. Wealth is loved more than son for one's own sake.
2. One self is loved more not for the sake of wealth.

So, Self is loved more.

In this way I am the object of Supreme Love is to be known.

Q. 184: How to know the gradation of love?

Ans: 1. In the waking state, the wealth is object of love. For the sake of wealth, a person leaves the country and goes abroad and engages in any kind of work. Thus, wealth is the object of love.

2. Son is more loved than the wealth. It is said that when one's son is caught for a wrong deed by the ruler then lot of wealth is offered to rescue the son. So, more than wealth, son is the object of love.
3. Body is more loved than the son. In time of adversity, son is sold to protect one's own body. So, more than the son, the body is the object of love.
4. The sense-organs are loved more than the body. It is said when someone attacks, the senses are protected and one says: "You can afflict my body but not eye, ear, nose, face, etc.". So, more than body, the sense-organs are the object of love.
5. The vital air (mind) is more loved than sense-organs. It is said when a person due to illegal action is summoned by the king who says "take his life" the culprit pleads "take away my wealth, son, wife, house, etc., but don't take away my life". When the king

orders for a death sentence then the convict pleads "cut my ear, cut my nose, cut my hand, cut my leg but don't take my life". So, vital air is more loved than sense-organs.

6. Self is loved more than vital air. It is said when someone is extremely ill due to fatal disease such a one says "I am happy if my life ends". So, Self is more loved than vital air.

In this way, the gradation of love is to be known.

Thus ends the eighth digit of *Vicāracandrodaya* titled "Existence, Consciousness, Absolute Happiness".

Kalā 9

Indescribability

इन्द्रविजय छंद (*Indravijaya* Metre)

ब्रह्म अहै मनबानि-अगोचर।
शास्त्र रु संत कहैं अरु ध्यावैं॥

वेद बदें लछनादिकरीति रु
वृत्ति विआप्ति जनो मन लावैं॥

हैं जु सदादिविधेयविशेषण।
वे असदादिक भिन्न कहावैं॥

सत्य अपेक्षिक आदि विरोधि जु
अंस तजी परमार्थ लखावैं॥ १८ ॥

हैं जु अनंत अखंड असंग रु
अद्वयआदिनिषेध्य रहावैं॥

वे परपंच निषेध करी अव-
शेषितवस्तु गिराबिन गावैं॥

यूं परमातम आतम देवही।
वेद रु शास्त्र सबे सुरटावैं॥

पंडित त्यागि अभास पीतांबर।
वृत्ति अहं अपरोक्षहि पावैं॥ १९ ॥

brahma ahai manabāni-agocara।
śāstra ru santa kahaiṅ aru dhyāvaiṅ॥

veda badeṅ lachanādikarīti ru।
vṛtti viāpti jano mana lāvaiṅ॥

haiṅ ju sadādividheyaviśeṣaṇa।
ve asadādika bhinna kahāvaiṅ॥

satya apekṣika ādi virodhi ju ।
aṅsa tajī paramārtha lakhāvaiṅ ।। 18 ।।

haiṅ ju ananta akhaṇḍa asaṅga ru ।
advaya ādiniṣedhya rahāvaiṅ ।।

ve parapañca niṣedha karī ava-
śeṣitavastu girābina gāvaiṅ ।।

yūṅ paramātama ātama devahī ।
veda ru śāstra sabe suraṭāvaiṅ ।।

paṇḍita tyāgi abhāsa pītāṁbara ।
vr̥tti ahaṁ aparokṣahi pāvaiṅ ।। 19 ।।

Brahman is incomprehensible by mind and words,
is enquired into by scriptures and
noble ones teach and meditate.

Vedas reveal through secondary implication and
by pervasion of thought, bring into mind
the direct definition like Existence
they reveal the contrary like non-existence,
the relative truth etc.,[144] that are contrary
aspects, the absolute truth[145] is known through
the secondary implication ।। 18 ।।

That which is infinite, indivisible, relationless and
non-dual, etc. remain as negators.

They negate the universe, the remaining
entity is proclaimed as indescribable.

Paramātmā and *ātmā* are differentiators
in Vedas and scriptures, everything is

---

144 Relative truth, knowledge in the form of thought and happiness through sense-organs etc. are contrary aspects. These are to be given up.

145 The absolute truth, knowledge in the form of Consciousness and the *ānanda* nature of Self, etc. are to be known through the secondary implication.

given up by the scholar[146] as reflection, Pitambar
gains the thought-modification of I as direct || 19 ||

Q. 185: When *Brahmātmā* is not describable by words then how can adjectives like Existence, Consciousness, Absolute Happiness be used? [See also Q. 141.]

Ans: The features of *Brahmātmā* are in the form of *vidheya viśeṣaṇa*[147] and *niṣedha viśeṣaṇa*.[148] Of these,

1. the *vidheya* features are Existence etc., which negate the world and point out to the remainder as *Brahman* revealing directly through the secondary signification.[149]

---

146 Scholar or *paṇḍit* refers to reflection (pervasion by reflected consciousness), which is given up, and the I-thought (pervasion by thought) is known directly. This is the meaning.

147 *Brahman*, revealed by words like "Existence" and "Consciousness" that are direct, is known as *vidheya viśeṣaṇa*.

148 *Brahman*, revealed by words of negation like "without end" and "without division", is known as *niṣedha viśeṣaṇa*.

149 [1] (*Vācyārtha* — primary meaning): *Māyā* and the world are extrinsically real and *Brahman* is intrinsically real. They together form the primary meaning of the word "Existence". (*Lakṣyārtha* — secondary meaning). In secondary signification, the reality of *māyā* is given up and the reality of only *Brahman* is retained.

[2] (*Vāc*): The knowledge in the form of thought in the mind and Consciousness in the form of knowledge, they together form the primary meaning of the word "Consciousness".

(*Lak*): In secondary signification, the knowledge as thought-mode is given up and the knowledge as nature of Consciousness is retained.

[3] (*Vāc*): Happiness through sense object, happiness through impressions and nature of *Brahman* as Absolute Happiness, all these three together are the primary meaning of the word "Absolute Happiness".

(*Lak*): In secondary meaning by giving up of the two, the nature of *Brahman* as Absolute Happiness is retained.

→

2. The *niṣedha* features are Limitlessness, etc. and these directly negate the world and here *Brahman* is revealed by secondary signification. Really, *Brahmātmā* is indescribable; it cannot be revealed by any adjective.

→ [4] (*Vāc*): *Māyā* and its effects like space are of relative pervasiveness and *Brahman* (Self) is of absolute pervasiveness. They together form the primary meaning of the word *Brahman* (Big).

(*Lak*): Only *Brahman* forms the secondary meaning of the word *Brahman*.

[5] (*Vāc*): The reflected consciousness in the mind possesses relative self-luminosity whereas Consciousness is of absolute self-luminosity. These two form the primary meaning of the word "Self-luminous".

(*Lak*): Consciousness alone is meant in the secondary meaning of the word "Self-luminous".

[6] (*Vāc*): Rope etc. are relative non-modifiers and Consciousness is the absolute non-modifier. Both constitute the primary meaning of the word "unchanging" (*kūṭastha*).

(*Lak*): Retaining only Consciousness is secondary meaning of Unchanging.

[7] (*Vāc*): The primary meaning of the word "witness" includes the empirical witness principle and *māyā–avidyā* conditioning Consciousness (*Brahman* and *ātman*).

(*Lak*): The Consciousness conditioned by *māyā* is retained as the "witness" principle in secondary signification.

[8] (*Vāc*): The primary meaning of the word Seer includes the thought form in the mind with reflected consciousness which perceives because of Consciousness.

(*Lak*): The Consciousness part alone is referred to in the secondary signification.

[9] (*Vāc*): The onlooker of the ritual and the inner self, both are included in the primary meaning of the word Onlooker.

(*Lak*): The inner self alone is referred to in the secondary meaning of the word Onlooker.

[10] (*Vāc*): The word One primarily includes one person as known in the world and *Brahman* is devoid of homogeneous difference etc.

→

Q. 186: How does the *vidheya* features like *sat* negate the world and arrive at the remainder as *Brahman*?

Ans: 1. By saying "Existence", the non-existence is negated, then what remains is Existence and this gets established by secondary signification.

2. By stating "Consciousness", the matter gets negated, then what remains is Consciousness and this gets established by secondary signification.

3. "Absolute Happiness" dismisses sorrow and what remains is Absolute Happiness and this gets established by secondary meaning.

4. The word *Brahman* negates limitations and what remains is the all-pervasive entity and this gets established by secondary signification.

5. The word "Self-luminous" negates dependently luminous ones and what remains is the self-luminous entity which is attained by secondary meaning.

6. The word "Stable" (unmodifying) negates the changing and what remains is the unmodified one and this is known secondarily.

7. "Witness principle" negates the witnessed and what remains is the witness known through the secondary meaning.

8. "Seer" negates the seen and remainder is the Seer known by secondary derivation.

9. "Onlooker" negates the onlooked, i.e. the proximate entities are negated and what remains is the Onlooker by secondary meaning.

→ (*Lak*): The word One secondarily signifies only *Brahman*.

In this way the other unsaid *vidheya* features are to be known.

In this manner, the *niṣedha* features like Existence contrary to non-existence are also to be known by this method of *bhāga-tyāga-lakṣaṇā*.

10. By stating "One", the "many" are dismissed and what remains is One. This is known by secondary signification.

In this way, the other *vidheya* features are to be known.

Q. 187: How do the *niṣedha* features like Limitlessness negate the world?

Ans: The word Limitlessness means that which is not limited by space, time or another entity. What remains is Limitlessness and this is known by the very meaning. In this way, the other *niṣedha* features are to be known.

Q. 188: What is the purpose of deriving such a meaning for these features?

Ans: The purpose of deriving such a meaning for these features is that in the revelation of scriptures as Consciousness being not an object of mind or words is understood without contradiction. The means that operate in the field of words and mind are quality, action, class and relation, and these are not in *Brahman*. *Brahman* is free from such features and is devoid of specificities. Hence, scriptures say *Brahman* is not the object of mind and words.

Moreover, what is described leads to duality and not non-duality. Therefore when these features are known in this manner they will not contradict scriptural statement and will not lead to duality, also non-duality can be easily comprehended.

Thus ends the ninth digit of *Vicāracandrodaya* titled "Indescribability".

Kalā 10

General and Specific Consciousnesses

इंद्रविजय छंद (*Indravijaya* Metre)

चेतन हैं जु समान विशेष सु।
दोविधसत्य सुजान समानै।।

भ्रांति सरूप विशेष जु कल्पित।
संसृति आश्रय सो तिहि भानै।।

ज्या रविको प्रतिबिंब जलादिक।
सो रविरूप विशेष पिछानै।।

त्यों मतिमैं प्रतिबिंब परातम।
सो कलपीत विशेषहिं जानै।। २० ।।

आवत जावत लोक प्रलोक हिं।
भोगत भोग जु कर्म निपानै।।

सो सब चित-अभास करे अरु।
शुद्धि समान महीं नहिं आनै।।

अस्ति रु भाति प्रियं सब पूरन-
ब्रह्म समान सु चेतन मानै।।

नाम रु रूप तजी सत् चेतन।
मोद पीतांबर आप पिछानै।। २१ ।।

cetana haiṁ ju samāna viśeṣa su।
dovidhasatya sujāna samānai।।

bhrāṅti sarūpa viśeṣa ju kalpita।
saṁsṛti āśraya so tihi bhānai।।

jyā raviko pratibiṁba jalādika।
so ravirūpa viśeṣa pichānai।।

tyoṅ matimaiṅ pratibiṁba parātama ।
so kalapīta viśeṣahiṅ jānai ।। 20 ।।

āvata jāvata loka praloka hiṅ ।
bhogata bhoga ju karma nipānai ।।

so saba cita-abhāsa kare aru ।
śuddha samāna mahīṁ nahiṅ ānai ।।

asti ru bhāti priyaṁ saba pūrana-
brahma samāna su cetana mānai ।।

nāma ru rūpa tajī sat cetana ।
moda pītāṁbara āpa pichānai ।। 21 ।।

Consciousness is General and specific,
results in two kinds of truths.

Delusion is the nature of specific which is imagined,
is the support of bondage that illumines,
as sun's reflection on water etc.
is the form of sun which is specific.

Similarly, in the mind there is reflection[150] *paramātmā*,
it is to be known as the imagined specific ।। 20 ।।

Appears and disappears into world and other worlds,
experiences are varied due to *karma*.[151]

These are semblance of Consciousness[152]
that are not pure like the original.

Existence, Knowledge, Love everything is complete —
Brahman and Consciousness are to be known as the same.

The name and form are to be excluded,
Existence, Consciousness, Love,
are to be recognized as Pitambar ।। 21 ।।

---

150 It is reflection of *Paramātmā*.

151 The results caused by *karma* are experienced.

152 Reflection of Consciousness.

Q. 189: What is specific consciousness?

Ans: The reflection of General Consciousness *Brahman* in the mind and thoughts is called as specific consciousness.[153]

Q. 190: What is the definition of reflected consciousness?

Ans: 1. Is different from the definition of Consciousness (*Brahman*) and

2. illumines like Consciousness.

This is reflected consciousness.

Q. 191: Why is reflected consciousness known as specific consciousness?

Ans: That which is limited in space and time is said to be "specific".[154] The reflected consciousness is in the mind and also during the waking, dream and ignorant states; so it is known as "specific consciousness".

Q. 192: What is the example for specific consciousness?

Ans: 1. Just as the light of the sun spreads everywhere but does not get reflected everywhere but only where there are adjuncts like water and mirror, it reflects and shines specifically.

2. Or, as the light of the sun is same everywhere and does not burn things like cloth, cotton, etc., but through

---

153 The specific consciousness, which is described here as the reflected consciousness, is the one which was introduced as "imagined specific part" in the sixth digit [see Q. 126].

154 The specific in the form of "substratum" and "superimposed" is of two types. Of which,

(1) during the time of delusion, that which is not known but by its knowledge the delusion is eliminated, it is the specific kind of the nature of substratum and

(2) that which is perceived during the time of delusion and which is not perceived on the knowledge of the substratum, is the superimposed form of specific. This alone is also known as imagined specific.

the lens it assumes the special form of fire and burns cloth and cotton.

1. General form is that which is always as it is (for a long time).
2. When it shines through an adjunct it is specific. This is variable and unstable (remains for some time).

1. The nature of Existence, Illumination and Love of the General Consciousness is present equally everywhere. But by this, there are no activities like speaking and walking.
2. Where there is the adjunct in the form of internal organ [mind] it contains the specific consciousness and because of reflection there is activity like speaking, walking, doer, enjoyer and movement in this and the other worlds.

Of which,

1. the General Consciousness which is *Brahman* is real and
2. the specific consciousness that shines in the limiting factor is reflection which is false.

Like,

1. doer of merits and demerits
2. enjoyer of pleasure and pain
3. movement in this world and the other worlds
4. birth and death
5. assuming lakhs of wombs.

Q. 193: What is to be ascertained by knowing the specific consciousness?

Ans: 1. the specific consciousness is reflection

2. that possesses qualities.

I am not this and it is not mine. But they are superimposed on Me. I am the General Consciousness, the substratum and different from it. This is to be ascertained.

Q. 194: What is General Consciousness?

Ans: 1. that which is all-pervasive like space

2. that which is the substratum of all names and forms
3. that which is of the nature of Existence, Illumination and Love
4. that which is Changeless *Brahman*

That is General Consciousness.

Q. 195: Why is *Brahman* referred to as the General Consciousness?

Ans: That which pervades more space and time is known as "general". *Brahman* pervades the entire space and time superimposed by mind. Therefore, *Brahman* is known as the General Consciousness.

Q. 196: What is the example by which the General Consciousness is known?

Ans: Example: Just as one rope is seen by different people as either a stick, or snake, or crack on the ground, or streak of water. This delusion has two parts.

1. one is the general "this" part
2. the other is the specific part which is expressed as,

[1] 1. "this" is a stick
2. "this" is a snake
3. "this" is a crack on the ground
4. "this" is a streak of water

In this way, the "this" part along with "snake" etc. is the general part which pervades everything. It is the general "this" part which

[1] illumines during the time of delusion also

[2] even after the removal of delusion "this is rope" in this manner it illumines.

Thus, the general "this" part is invariable and hence real.

[2] the snake etc. are specific parts that are mutually different and imagined.

Explanation: In every entity there are five aspects — (1) existence, (2) illumination, (3) love, (4) name, and (5) form

1. "this is pot", is existence [real]
2. "this pot is known", is illumination [consciousness]
3. "this pot is good"; the pot is useful for filling water and hence becomes an object of love (happiness). The snake or lion also are object of love for she-snake and lioness [respectively].
4. "pot" is (two letter *ghaṭa*) a name.
5. hard, round, big, are its forms.

In this way the entire element and the effects of elements are to be known. These reveal the five aspects of the external world.

1. In the case of body etc. that are internal

   [1] "I am" is existence

   [2] "I know" is illumination

   [3] "I am liked by another" is love

   [4] body, sense-organ, vital air, mind, intellect, memory, ego, ignorance and their features — these are names.

   [5] their respective shape is the form.

   These reveal the five aspects of the internal.

2. By giving up name and form of everything —

   [1] "this is earth"

   [2] "the earth shines — is known"

[3] "the earth is liked"; since earth gives the place for residing

[4] "earth" — is the name

[5] "possesses quality of smell" is its form.

3. By giving up name and form of earth —

[1] "this is water"

[2] "the water shines — is known"

[3] "the water is liked"; since water quenches thirst

[4] "water" — is the name

[5] "possesses quality of cold touch" is its form.

4. By giving up name and form of water —

[1] "this is fire"

[2] "the fire shines — is known"

[3] "the fire is liked"; since fire removes cold and darkness

[4] "fire" — is the name

[5] "possesses quality of hot touch" is its form.

5. By giving up name and form of fire —

[1] "this is air"

[2] "the air shines — is known"

[3] "the air is liked"; since air removes sweat

[4] "air" — is the name

[5] "possesses quality of touch without colour" is its form.

6. By giving up name and form of air —

[1] "this is space"

[2] "the space shines — is known"

[3] "the space is liked"; since space provides scope for moving about

[4] "space" — is the name

[5] "possesses quality of sound" is its form.

7. By giving up name and form of space —

[1] "what is behind is not known", is ignorance

[2] "ignorance is known"

[3] "ignorance is loved"; the ignorant one loves life, and ignorance is the cause of the world, the ignorant one maintains the life.

[4] "ignorance" — is the name

[5] "possesses concealment and projection power, is beginningless, indescribable and a positive entity" — are its form.

8. By giving up name and form of ignorance —

[1] "there is nothing" such knowledge of absence of an object is non-existence

[2] "non-existence is known"

[3] "non-existence is loved"; the school of "Nothingness" and "Meditators" are fond of non-existence

[4] "non-existence" — is the name

[5] "absence of all objects" (is the content of revelation of negation) — is its form.

9. By giving up name and form of absence —

[1] The nature of non-existence in the form of substratum, which is Existence, remains.

[2] It reveals the absence of non-existence, is Consciousness.

[3] Is different from sorrow; is Absolute Happiness.

In this way,

1. the invariable immanent substratum *Brahman* in every

name and form is the General Consciousness.[155] It is real and

2. the name and form of pot are not in cloth; the name and form of cloth are not in pot.

Thus there is mutual variability[156] and hence name and form are unreal.

This is the example to know the General Consciousness.

Q. 197: How is the above-mentioned *Brahman* of the form of General Consciousness said to be more subtle and pervasive?

Ans: 1. The effects are gross and limited.

2. The cause is subtle and pervasive (pervades more space). This is the rule.

Brahman is the cause of everything and hence is more subtle and pervasive. This is shown:

(1) [1] From the ocean water are formed foam and salt. This

---

[155] (1) The General Consciousness is the illuminator of deep sleep, swooning and *samādhi*.

(2) "I know the pot" in this way the knower, means of knowledge and the object of knowledge, this triad is illumined by the witness principle which is the General Consciousness.

(3) The junctions of the three states like waking are revealed by the General Consciousness.

(4) General Consciousness reveals the unity of flow of thoughts.

(5) General Consciousness reveals up to the tip of the thumb.

(6) The awareness of the junction between the wandering thoughts is made known by the General Consciousness.

(7) The junction between two thoughts like that of sun and moon is also made known by the General Consciousness.

(8) "I don't know myself" such an ignorance of myself is also illumined by the General Consciousness.

[156] That which is present at times and not present at other times is said to be variable.

shows that earth is the product of water. Compared to earth, water is subtle and pervasive. Or,

[2] the parts of the earth like stone etc., when tied in a cloth do not fall

[3] the water cannot be contained in a cloth

[4] when earth is dug there is water

[5] in Purāṇas, water is said to be ten times more pervasive than earth.

For these reasons also water is subtle and pervasive than earth.

(2) [1] By the heat of fire there is sweat in the body. Water is the effect of fire. Fire is subtle and pervasive than water. Or,

[2] water is not contained in cloth, but water remains in pot

[3] the light of sun, etc. do not remain in pot

[4] in Purāṇas, fire is said to be ten times more pervasive than water.

For these reasons also fire is subtle and pervasive than water.

(3) [1] The origin and extinguishing of fire are based on air. Fire is a product of air. Air is subtle and pervasive than fire. Or,

[2] the light of sun etc. are not contained in a pot, but is seen with eyes, but air cannot be seen with eyes.

[3] In Purāṇas, air is said to be ten times more pervasive than fire.

For these reasons also, air is subtle and pervasive than fire.

(4) [1] The origin, sustenance and resolution of air cannot happen without space. Air is product of space. Space is subtle and pervasive. Or,

[2] air cannot be seen with eyes, but is known by the sense

of touch but space cannot be known by the sense of touch.

[3] In Purāṇas, space is said to be ten times more pervasive than air.

For these reasons also, space is subtle and pervasive than air.

(5) [1] One may ponder over "what is above space?", the reply may be "I don't know" — the ignorance in mind is revealed. Space is the product of ignorance. Ignorance is subtle and pervasive. Or,

[2] space cannot be known by the sense of touch, but can be known by mind and ignorance is not known by mind also.

[3] Scriptures say that ignorance is infinitely pervasive than space.

So, ignorance is subtle and pervasive than space.

(6) [1] The experience of ignorance expressed as "I don't know" is know because of Consciousness.

1. There is ignorance

2. That there is ignorance is known

3. Ignorance is perpetuated by the ignorant ones.

In this manner, the *Brahman* Consciousness in the form of Existence, Illumination and Love pervades ignorance. Ignorance is supported by Consciousness. *Brahman* Consciousness is subtle and pervasive than ignorance. Or,

[2] ignorance is not known by mind, but is inferred by the reason "I don't know". *Brahman* Consciousness being Self-luminous does not require any means of knowledge.

[3] Like a mole in the body, ignorance remains in Consciousness. The remainder *Brahman* is of Pure Self-luminosity. This is revealed by the scriptures.

For these reasons also, *Brahman* is subtle and pervasive than ignorance.

Q. 198: What is to be ascertained by knowing the General Consciousness?

Ans:(1) [1] I am *Brahman*, the General Consciousness which is Existence, Illumination and Love.

[2] I am the General Consciousness *Brahman* of the nature of Existence, Illumination and Love.

(2) The world of name and form is superimposed on Me. This is to be ascertained.

Q. 199: What is attained by such a determination?

Ans: If this is ascertained in this manner then all sorrows are removed and there is attainment of absolute happiness which is liberation.

Thus ends the tenth digit of *Vicāracandrodaya* titled "General and Specific Consciousnesses".

Kalā 11

Establishment of Oneness of the Word-meanings of Tat and Tvam

इंद्रविजय छंद (*Indravijaya* Metre)

वाच्य रु लक्ष्य लखी तत्‌-त्वंपद।
लक्ष्य दुहूंकर एक दृढावै॥

भिन्न जु देशहि काल सु वस्तु रु।
धर्मसमेत उपाधि उडावै॥

जन्म थिती लय कारक मायिक।
जाननहार सबी जग भावै॥

ईश्वर वाच्य सु है ततपादहि।
ब्रह्म सु लक्ष्य उपाधि अभावै॥ २२ ॥

संसृति मानत आपहिमैं पर-
तंत्र अविद्यक अल्प जनावै॥

त्वंपद वाच्य सु जीव विवेचित।
लक्ष्य सु साक्षि उपाधि ढहावै॥

वाच्य दुअर्थ हि भेद बि है पुनि।
लक्ष्य विभेद न रंचक गावै॥

ब्रह्म अहं इस भांति जु जानत।
सोई पीतांबर ब्रह्महि पावै॥ २३ ॥

vācya ru lakṣya lakhī tat-tvaṁpada।
lakṣya duhūṁkara eka dṛḍhāvai॥

bhinna ju deśahi kāla su vastu ru।
dharmasameta upādhi uḍāvai॥

janma thitī laya kāraka māyika।
jānanahāra sabī jaga bhāvai॥

īśvara vācya su hai tatapādahi ।
brahma su lakṣya upādhi abhāvai ।। 22 ।।

saṁsr̥ti mānata āpahimaiṁ para-
tantra avidyaka alpa janāvai ।।

tvaṁpada vācya su jīva vivecita ।
lakṣya su sākṣi upādhi ḍhahāvai ।।

vācya duartha hi bheda bi hai puni ।
lakṣya vibheda na rañcaka gāvai ।।

brahma ahaṁ isa bhāṅti ju jānata ।
soī pītāṁbara brahmahi pāvai ।। 23 ।।

There are primary and secondary meanings
for *tat* and *tvam* words,
the oneness is ascertained through secondary meaning.

Differences due to space, time and as entity,
along with attributive adjunct are blown off.

Birth, sustenance and resolution, with factor *māyika,*[157]
evolve the perceptible world.

The primary sense is *Īśvara* denoted by the word *tat*
Brahman is the implied sense in absence of the adjunct ।। 22 ।।

The individual self is seen as bound, dependent
micro-ignorance,[158] limited by knowledge.
The [primary] meaning of the word
tvam is *jīva,* which is to be discriminated
by implied sense as witness, eliminating the adjunct.

The primary sense shows the difference again,
secondary sense reveals that there is no difference.

"I am *Brahman*" if this is known,
Pitambar, attains *Brahman* ।। 23 ।।

---

157 One with the adjunct of *māyā*.

158 One with the adjunct of *avidyā*.

Q. 200: What is the word *tat* [that]?

Ans: In the sixth chapter of *Chāndogya Upaniṣad* belonging to *Sāmaveda*, Uddālaka the father instructed his son Śvetaketu *tat tvam asi*[159] *mahāvākya* and the first word here is *tat*.

Q. 201: What is the word *tvam* [you]?

Ans: It is the second word of the *tat tvam asi mahāvākya*.

Q. 202: What are its primary and secondary meanings?

Ans: The relation of the word with its meaning is known as *vṛtti* of the word. The *vṛtti* is of two kinds: 1. *śakti vṛtti*, and 2. *lakṣaṇā vṛtti*.

1. The capacity to gain the knowledge of the meaning by the word, where the word and its meaning have a direct relation, is called as *śakti vṛtti* of the word.
2. Through the meaning of the *śakti vṛtti* where the word is related to the meaning indirectly is known as *lakṣaṇā vṛtti* of the word.

In this,

1. the meaning of a word known by *śakti vṛtti* is called

---

159 (1) Like *tat tvam asi* [*Sāmaveda mahāvākya*].

(2) *Ṛgveda mahāvākya* is *prajñānam brahma*.

(3) *Yajurveda mahāvākya* is *aham brahmāsmi*.

(4) *Atharvaveda mahāvākya* is *ayamātmā brahma*.

[1] The primary meaning of the word *tat* is *Īśvara* and the secondary meaning is Pure *Brahman*. The word *brahma* in the above three *mahāvākya*s also has the same primary and secondary meanings.

[2] The primary meaning of the word *tvam* is *jīva* and the secondary meaning is the unchanging witness principle (*kūṭastha sākṣī*). The words *prajñānam, aham, ayam* with the word *ātmā* all the three *mahāvākya*s have the same primary and secondary meanings. By the *mahāvākya tat tvam asi* the oneness of *jīva* and *Brahman* is revealed, similarly the oneness is revealed through the other *mahāvākya*s.

primary meaning (*vācyārtha*). It is also known as *śakyārtha* and *mukhyārtha*.

2. the meaning of a word known through *lakṣaṇā vṛtti* is called secondary meaning (*lakṣyārtha*).

Q. 203: How many kinds of secondary meanings are there?

Ans: (1) Exclusive, (2) non-exclusive, and (3) exclusive–non-exclusive — these are the three kinds of secondary meanings.

Q. 204: What are the definition and example of these three secondary meanings?

Ans: 1. Where the entire primary meaning of the word is given up and the meaning related to the primary meaning is taken up is called exclusive secondary meaning (*jahallakṣaṇā*).

As someone asks a person, "where is the village of the cowherds?" and someone says "the village is on the Gaṅgā". The primary meaning of the word Gaṅgā refers to the flow of the sacred river. Here the entire primary meaning is given up that refers to the flow of the river and the related meaning to the primary meaning, that is "on the banks" is taken.

2. Where the primary meaning is not given up but its related meaning is included then it is called non-exclusive secondary meaning (*ajahallakṣaṇā*).

As someone said "the browns are running". Here the primary meaning of the word brown refers to the colour that cannot run. It refers [contextually] to the brown horse. Here, the primary meaning is not given up but a meaning related to it, i.e. the "horse", is included.

3. When a certain contradictory part in the primary meaning is given up and the related non-contradictory part in the primary meaning is retained it is called

exclusive–non-exclusive secondary meaning (*bhāga–tyāga-lakṣaṇā*).

Just as a person who has met the other, after a long time in a different place and time, sees the same person now in a different place and time says, "the person whom I met somewhere (past place) at some time (past time) is now (present time) in this place (present place)". The place and time of the past and present are contradictory, they are given up. "This is the same person", which is non-contradictory, is retained.

Q. 205: Of these three kinds of secondary meaning which is applied to the *mahāvākya*?

Ans: 1. In the exclusive secondary signification, the primary meaning is completely given up. If this is applied to the *mahāvākya* then,

[1] The *Brahman* Consciousness and the witness Consciousness that are included in the primary meaning also will have to be given up.

[2] Then the inert world of bondage has to be taken. Otherwise, the adjunct of the macro and the micro (the adjectival form of the primary part) also has to be given up with the Consciousness principle and what then will remain is "nothing".

By this one lands in adversity in which there is no goal to be accomplished. Hence the exclusive secondary signification cannot be applied to the *mahāvākya*.

2. In the non-exclusive secondary signification, the primary meaning is not given up but another meaning is included. If the *mahāvākya* is derived from this non-exclusive secondary meaning, then the primary meaning of the words *tat* and *tvam* will remain as it is and another meaning to be included will be only

nothingness. Here, the contradiction to oneness is not removed. Thus, there is no purpose by the application of this non-exclusive secondary meaning. So, this is also not applied in the case of the *mahāvākya*.

3. The exclusive–non-exclusive secondary meaning is where the contradictory features are given up and the non-contradictory feature is retained.
   [1] In the primary meaning of *tat* and *tvam*, the contradictory features are properties with *māyā–avidyā*, which have to be given up.
   [2] The non-contradicting unassociated, Pure Consciousness is to be retained.

So that,
   [1] by this the oneness is achieved.
   [2] the highest goal is also gained.

Thus, the exclusive–non-exclusive secondary meaning is applied to the *mahāvākya*.

Q. 206: What are the primary and secondary meanings of the word *tat*?

Ans: 1. The unmanifest *māyā* is the space principle of *Īśvara.*

2. The creation, sustenance and dissolution are the time principles of *Īśvara.*

3. The *sattva, rajas* and *tamas* are the entities[160] of *Īśvara.* They are the constituents of the creation.

---

[160] Even though *māyā* and the three qualities together are one entity and there is oneness of space, time and body of *Īśvara,* then also just as in the case of a potter who makes a pot,

(1) mud in the form of earth is the space

(2) the mud clod is the entity and

(3) the parts like bone etc. which are the parts of earth are the body whose oneness is not impossible. In the same way, the oneness of space etc. of *Īśvara* is also not impossible.

4. *Virāṭ, Hiraṇyagarbha* and *Avyākr̥ta* — these three are the bodies of *Īśvara.*

5. *Vaiśvānara, Sūtrātmā, Antaryāmī* — these three form the identification of *Īśvara.*

6. "I am one and shall become many" — beginning from such a visualization up to "and entered into the *jīva*" is [the description of] creation. This is the activity of *Īśvara*.

7. [1] Omnipotence, [2] Omniscience, [3] Omnipresence, [4] One, [5] Independent, [6] Skilful, [7] Indirectness, and [8] with the adjunct *māyā* — these eight are the qualities of *Īśvara*.

(1) [1] Along with these is *māyā* and

[2] in which there is the reflected consciousness and

[3] whose substratum is *Brahman.*

These put together are known as *Īśvara*. This is the primary meaning of the word *tat*.

(2) By giving up all these with *māyā* and the reflected consciousness, what remains is the substratum of *Virāṭ, Hiraṇyagarbha* and *Avyākr̥ta* that is *Īśvara sākṣī* Pure *Brahman* which is the secondary meaning of the word *tat*.

Q. 207: How does the mutual superimposition of *Brahman* and *Īśvara* which is the reflection on *māyā* take place?

Ans: On enquiry,

1. the reality of *Brahman* is superimposed on *Īśvara* due to relation of identity. By which *Īśvara* is seen as real.

2. *Īśvara* and the causal nature of *Īśvara* are superimposed on *Brahman*. By which, *Brahman* is seen as the cause of the universe. This is said to be (*anuvāda*) means of temporary definition (*taṭastha lakṣaṇā*) given in the

Śruti, Purāṇa and by preceptors. In this way, there is mutual superimposition of *Brahman* and *Īśvara*.

Q. 208: How is this error removed?

Ans: The above-mentioned error gets removed by discriminative knowledge.

Q. 209: What is the primary and secondary meaning of the word *tvam*?

Ans: 1. Eyes, neck and heart — these three are the places of *jīva*.

2. Waking, dream and deep sleep — these three are the times of *jīva*.

3. Gross, subtle and causal — these three are the materials of *jīva* (materials for experience).

4. This is the body

5. *Viśva, taijasa* and *prājña* — these three are the identifications of *jīva*.

6. Beginning from waking state up to liberation, the various experiences are *saṁsāra*. This is the activity of *jīva*.

7. [1] Limited power, [2] limited knowledge, [3] bound, [4] plurality, [5] dependence, [6] incapacity, [7] direct, and [8] with adjunct of *avidyā* — these eight are the properties of *jīva*.

(1) [1] All these with *avidyā* and

[2] in which there is the reflected consciousness

[3] whose substratum is *kūṭastha*.

All these together are known as *jīva*. This is the primary meaning of the word *tvam*.

(2) The reflected consciousness with these qualities is to be given up and what remains is the *kūṭastha jīva sākṣī*

which is the substratum of gross, subtle and causal bodies. This is the secondary meaning of the word *tvam*.

Q. 210: How does the superimposition take place between *kūṭastha* and *jīva* which is the reflection in the mind?

Ans: On enquiry,

1. due to relation of identity, the reality of *kūṭastha* is superimposed on *jīva*. So, *jīva* is not known as false but is seen as real.
2. *Jīva* and the property of *jīva* as doership, etc. are superimposed on *kūṭastha*.

Kūṭastha is not known as non-doer, non-reaper, non-bound, eternally free, unassociated, *Brahman* but is known contradictorily. In this way, there is the mutual superimposition of *kūṭastha* and *jīva*.

Q. 211: How is this error removed?

Ans: The above-mentioned error is removed by discriminative knowledge.

Q. 212: How is the oneness of *tat* and *tvam* as given in the *mahāvākya* arrived at?

Ans: 1. Even though the primary meaning of the words *tat* and *tvam* is Consciousness with limiting factor (*Īśvara* and *jīva*), whose oneness is contradictory,

2. then also secondary meaning of *tat* is *Brahman*, and *tvam* is *ātmā* and there is no contradiction in their oneness.

By bringing out the meaning of *tat* and *tvam* in the *mahāvākya* in this manner, the oneness is arrived at.

Q. 213: Who attains the knowledge of oneness and expresses "I am *Brahman*"?

Ans: This knowledge is attained in the reflected consciousness.

Q. 214: The reflected consciousness is different from *Brahman*, then how does one know the nature of *Brahman* as oneself?

Ans: 1. The *kūṭastha* which is the substratum of *jīva*-notion is primarily non-different from *Brahman*.

2. The reflected consciousness along with mind, being sublated, results in oneness of *Brahman*.

Or,

1. the reflected consciousness sublates its nature knowing the secondary meaning of the word "I" as *kūṭastha*.
2. The real nature of *kūṭastha* is expressed as "I am *kūṭastha*" with this identification it is known as "I am *Brahman*". In this manner, the reflected consciousness knows Self as *Brahman*.

Q. 215: What is the example to show the oneness of *tat* and *tvam* by secondary meaning?

Ans: Example

1. As,
   [1] the oneness of space confined within a pot and room known as pot-space and room-space is contradictory.
   [2] then also, without focusing on the pot or room, arriving at oneness of the space is not contradictory.
2. As,
   [1] flame glows in glass lamp and mud lamp. There is no oneness of the flame in these two containers.
   [2] then also, the fire of the flame is one, which is non-contradictory.
3. As,
   [1] the king and the shepherd whose adjuncts are army and sheep, their oneness is contradictory.
   [2] then also, the humanness is one, which is non-contradictory.

4. As,

   [1] there is Gaṅgā water and the container of Gaṅgā water. Their adjuncts are river and container whose oneness is contradictory.

   [2] then also, there is no contradiction in the oneness of only Gaṅgā water.

5. As,

   [1] Water is present in the form of ocean and wave. The adjuncts are ocean and wave whose oneness is contradictory.

   [2] There is oneness of only water where there is no contradiction.

6. As,

   [1] one person is known as son from the standpoint of father, and grandson from the standpoint of grandfather, based on these limiting factors their oneness is contradictory.

   [2] The oneness as the person in both is not contradictory.

7. There was a certain king in Kāśī. He travelled to other countries on an elephant so that the other travellers can see him. Once, a passer-by went to Kāśī and found that there was another king. The earlier king now moved about as a mendicant and reached another country. One who recognized him introduced to the other person that he was the king of Kāśī. The other person wondered:

   [1] The king's country is different. This is another country.

   [2] His time (status) was different, now his status is different.

   [3] His material was different, now it is something else.

   [4] His identification was different, now it is something else.

[5] His activity was different, now it is different.

[6] His property was different, now his property is different.

Then how can the king of Kāśī and this mendicant be the same?

The first traveller then says, by giving up the king's and this mendicant's (1) place, (2) time, (3) material, (4) identification, (5) activity, and (6) property, see the one person inherent in all these, the oneness is known.

Explanation: The place, time, etc. of *jīva* and *Īśvara* are given up and the inherent consciousness as *Brahman* and *ātman* in both is one. One should firmly ascertain "*Brahman* is me"; "I am *Brahman*". This is known as the knowledge of reality. This is in the form of removal of all sorrows and attainment of supreme peace which is called liberation.

Thus ends the eleventh digit of *Vicāracandrodaya* titled "Establishment of Oneness of the Word-meanings of Tat and Tvam".

Kalā 12

Destruction of Karma in the Enlightened

तोटक छंद (*Toṭaka* Metre[161])

जिन आतमरूप पयो जु भले।
तिस त्रैविधकर्म मिटें सकले।।

तम आवृत्ति आश्रित संचित ले।
निज बोध सु पावक सर्व जले।। २४ ।।

जड चेतन गांठ विभेद बले।
दृढराग दवेष कषाय गले।।

जलमैं जिम लिप्त न कंजदले।
परसे न अगामि जु कर्म मले।। २५ ।।

इस जन्म अरंभक कर्म फले।
सुखदु:खहि भोगत होत प्रले।।

इस भांति जु होवत जन्म विले।
पिख रूप पीतांबर स्वं विमले।। २६ ।।

jina ātamarūpa payo ju bhale
tisa traividhakarma miṭeṅ sakale

tama āvr̥tti āśrita sañcita le
nija bodha su pāvaka sarva jale 24

jaḍa cetana gāṅṭha vibheda bale
dr̥ḍharāga daveṣa kaṣāya gale

jalamaiṅ jima lipta na kañjadale
parase na agāmi ju karma male 25

---

161 This is sung prevalently in *ṭhumarī*.

isa janm̥a araṁbhaka karma phale ।
sukhaduḥkhahi bhogata hota prale ।।

isa bhāṅti ju hovata janma vile ।
pikha rūpa pītāṁbara svaṁ vimale ।। 26 ।।

The nature of Self when gained,[162]
the three kinds of results of action all get erased.

Enveloped by ignorance[163] rest the
past accumulated results, beginning from that
everything is burnt by the fire of Self-knowledge ।। 24 ।।

The knot of difference between inert and sentient is present,
firm dispassion is medicine for the poison in throat.

Untouched by water is the leaf in pond,[164]
remains unaffected by the future results of action ।। 25 ।।

The fructified results of this birth,
are exhausted through experiences of pleasure and pain.

The birth which is to happen like this, resolves,
seen[165] form Pitambar Self is pure ।। 26 ।।

Q. 216: What is *karma*?

Ans: The activity performed through body, speech and mind is called *karma*.

Q. 217: How many types of *karma* are there?

Ans: (1) *Sañcita,* (2) *prārabdha,* and (3) *āgāmī* are the three types of *karma*.

Q. 218: What is *sañcita karma*?

Ans: (1) The result of action performed in countless past births is *sañcita karma*.

---

162 Known.

163 Beginning from *sañcita karma* that is supported by the power of concealment of ignorance [all *karma*s].

164 Lotus-leaf.

165 Recognized.

Q. 219: What is *prārabdha karma*?

Ans: (2) One of the fructified results of the many *sañcita karma*s and the beginning of the present body by the desire of *Īśvara* is known as *prārabdha karma*.

Q. 220: What is *āgāmī karma*?

Ans: (3) The action performed before or after attainment of knowledge through the present body until death is known as *āgāmī karma*.

Q. 221: How is the *karma* of an enlightened person eliminated?

Ans: 1. By knowledge, the concealment of ignorance is removed. By the removal of concealment, the result of action of past countless births, viz. the *sañcita* which is the support of concealment is removed (destroyed).

2. The *āgāmī karma* performed before and after knowledge through the present body is removed by the power of ascertained knowledge that "I am non-doer, non-reaper, unassociated, infinite". By this conviction, the delusion-born identity which is the support [of *āgāmī*] is destroyed and due to the absence of likes and dislikes, like the water in lotus-leaf, the enlightened remains untouched. But, the meritorious *āgāmī karma* of the wise person in the present birth goes to the noble ones and the demeritorious *āgāmī karma* of the wise person goes to those who hate him.

3. The *prārabdha karma* of the wise person is supported by the *vikṣepa* of the ignorant one. *Prārabdha* is the fructification of the *karma* of past birth that gets removed by the experience of the *karma* [its result] in the present birth. Thus, the wise person is free from all *karma*s. Thereby, the wise person is free from this bondage of birth, etc., which is the result of *karma*.

Thus ends the twelfth digit of *Vicāracandrodaya* titled "Destruction of Karma in the Enlightened".

Kalā 13

The Seven Jñāna Bhūmikās

तोटक छंद (*Toṭaka* Metre)

निज बोधकि भूमि सु सप्त अहैं।
इस भांति वसिष्ठ मुनीश कहैं।।

शुभसाधन संपति आदि लहै।
श्रवणादिविचार द्वितीय वहै।। २७ ।।

निदिध्यासन तीसरभूमि गहै।
अपरोक्ष निजातम चौथि चहै।।

हमता ममता बिन पंचम है।
छटवी सब वस्तु अकार दहै।। २८ ।।

सतमी तुरिया जु वरिष्ठित है।
सबवृत्ति विलीन चिदात्म रहै।।

इव गाढसुषुप्ति न जागत है।
परमानंद मत्त पीतांबर है।। २९ ।।

nija bodhaki bhūmi su sapta ahaiṅ ।
isa bhāṅti vasiṣṭha munīśa kahaiṅ ।।

śubhasādhana saṁpati ādi lahai ।
śravaṇādivicāra dvitīya vahai ।। 27 ।।

nididhyāsana tīsarabhūmi gahai ।
aparokṣa nijātama cauthi cahaiḥ ।।

hamatā mamatā bina pañcama hai ।
chaṭavī saba vastu akāra dahaiḥ ।। 28 ।।

satamī turiyā ju variṣṭhita hai ।
sabavṛtti vilīna cidātma rahai ।।

iva gāḍhasuṣupti na jāgata hai ।
paramānanda matta pītāṁbara hai ।। 29 ।।

Self-knowledge has seven *bhūmikā*s,
this is said by Sage Vasiṣṭha.[166]

Wealth of refined means is the first stage,
Enquiry through *śravaṇa*, etc. is the second || 27 ||

Nididhyāsana is the third stage,
Direct knowledge of Self is the fourth.

Devoid of I-ness and mine-ness is the fifth,
Sixth is giving up of forms of all objects || 28 ||

Seventh is *turīya* which is higher,
where all thoughts resolve and Consciousness alone remain.

As[167] deep-sleep, there is no world,
is Absolute Peace Self Pitambar || 29 ||

Q. 222: It is said that the conviction of all wise persons is same, but is there a difference in the state (*sthiti*)?

Ans: The difference in the state of all wise persons is based on *jñāna-bhūmikā*.

Q. 223: What is *jñāna-bhūmikā*?

Ans: (1) *Śubha icchā,* (2) *suvicāraṇā,* (3) *tanumānasā,* (4) *sattvāpatti,* (5) *asaṁsakti,* (6) *padārthābhāvinī,* and (7) *turīyagā*. These are the seven *jñāna-bhūmikā*s.

Q. 224: What is *śubha icchā*?

Ans: (1) The four means — discrimination, dispassion, sixfold mental disciplines and desire for liberation — attained by *niṣkāma karma* and *upāsanā* giving rise to refinement and concentration, done either in the past birth or present birth, gives intense desire for knowledge of Self is known as *śubha icchā*. This is the first *bhūmikā* of *jñāna*.

---

166 In the text *Yoga-Vāsiṣṭha*.

167 Like deep sleep.

Q. 225: What is *suvicāraṇā*?

Ans: (2) By the intense desire for Self-knowledge, one approaches as prescribed [in the scriptures] and receives the teaching from a *guru* and listens to the oneness of *jīva* and *Brahman* through the Vedāntic statements. Then the doubt in the meaning of the statements listened to is removed by reasoning. This is known as *suvicāraṇā*, the second *bhūmikā* of *jñāna*.

Q. 226: What is *tanumānasā*?

Ans: (3) The gross or outward mind becomes subtle or inward by constant remembrance of the oneness of *Brahman–ātman* in *nididhyāsana*, the knowledge that has been ascertained through *śravaṇa* and *manana* as direct, is known as *tanumānasā*, the third *bhūmikā* of *jñāna*.

Q. 227: What is *sattvāpatti*?

Ans: (4) The direct revelation is the state devoid of differences attained by removal of doubt and contradiction through *śravaṇa, manana* and *nididhyāsana*. The refinement of mind attained by this knowledge of reality is known as *sattvāpatti*, the fourth *bhūmikā* of *jñāna*.

Q. 228: What is *asaṁsakti*?

Ans: (5) Through the constant practice of *nirvikalpa samādhi* there is maturity by which the I-ness and mine-ness with reference to the body are eliminated. There is absence of attachment with the body. This is known as *asaṁsakti*, which is the fifth *bhūmikā* of *jñāna*.

Q. 229: What is *padārthābhāvinī*?

Ans: (6) By the intense practice of *nirvikalpa samādhi*, there is the revelation of *Brahman* as the substratum of body by which non-existence is not arrived at. This is known as *padārthābhāvinī*, the sixth *bhūmikā* of *jñāna*.

Q. 230: What is *turīyagā*?

Ans: (7) The *tripuṭī* in the form of knower, known and knowledge — which is existent in fourth and fifth *bhūmikā*s and is non-existent in sixth *bhūmikā* — is not found here — this higher state of mind is known as *turīyagā*, the seventh *bhūmikā* of *jñāna*.

Q. 231: These seven *bhūmikā*s form the means of which aspects?

Ans: (1-3) The first, second and third *bhūmikā*s are means of knowledge of reality.

(4) The fourth *bhūmikā*[168] is the means for *jīvanmukti* and *videhamukti*, the result of Self-knowledge.

(5-7) Fifth, sixth and seventh *bhūmikā*s are the means for happiness other than that of *jīvanmukti*.

Thus ends the thirteenth digit of *Vicāracandrodaya* titled "The Seven Jñāna Bhūmikās".

---

168 (1) Performance of total meditation prior to knowledge is known as *kṛtopāsanā*.

(2) Non-performance of meditation prior to knowledge is known as *akṛtopāsanā*.

From this standpoint, the *adhikārī* of knowledge of the fourth *bhūmikā* is of two kinds. Of which,

(1) the *kṛtopāsaka* is one who possesses intense dispassion and other means to knowledge, that after the rise of knowledge without much effort, such a one elevates to the fifth *bhūmikā*.

(2) for the *akṛtopāsaka*, all means are not of high degree but only one or two means are attained and other means are hidden. One who is intelligent, gains the knowledge of truth in the form of fourth *bhūmikā* but after intense effort put forth for a long time, sometimes may reach the fifth *bhūmikā*, it is not immediate.

Kalā 14

Jīvanmukti and Videhamukti

तोटक छंद (*Toṭaka* Metre)

जब जानत है निजरूपहिकूं।
तब जीवन्मुक्ति समीपहिकूं।।

भ्रमबंध निवृत्ति सदेहहिकूं।
सुखसंपति होवत गेहहिकूं।। ३० ।।

विदवान तजै इस देहहिकूं।
तव पावत मुक्ति विदेहहिकूं।।

तम लेश भजे सद नाशहिकूं।
तज देत प्रपंच अभासहिकूं।। ३१ ।।

सरिता इव सागर देशहिकूं।
चिनमात्र मिलाय विशेषहिकूं।।

चिद होय भजे अवशेषहिकूं।
नहिं जन्म पीतांबर शेषहिकूं।। ३२ ।।

saba jānata hai nijarūpahikūṅ ।
taba jīvanmukti samīpahikūṅ ।।

bhramabandha nivṛtti sadehahikūṅ ।
sukhasaṁpati hovata gehahikūṅ ।। 30 ।।

vidavāna tajai isa dehahikūṅ ।
taba pāvata mukti videhahikūṅ ।।

tama leśa bhaje sada nāśahikūṅ ।
taja deta prapañca abhāsahikūṅ ।। 31 ।।

saritā iva sāgara deśahikūṅ ।
cinamātra milāya viśeṣahikūṅ ।।

cida hoya bhaje avaśeṣahikūṅ ।
nahiṅ janma pītāṁbara śeṣahikūṅ ।। 32 ।।

On recognizing the nature of Self,
then liberation-while-living is attained.

Confusion, bondage is removed along with body,[169]
wealth of happiness is attained || 30 ||

Enlightened one, when gives up this body,
then attains liberation from the body.

There is the remnant of ignorance that is to be destroyed,
the given world is an appearance || 31 ||

As the waterway[170] flows to join the ocean,
merges with Pure Consciousness, the specific.[171]

There remains only Consciousness,
there is no birth remaining for Pitambar || 32 ||

Q. 232: What is *jīvanmukti*?

Ans: The world, consisting of body is seen as *Brahman*, is *jīvanmukti*.

Q. 233: What is the vision of the world in *jīvanmukti*?

Ans: Concealment and projection — these two are the powers of *avidyā*. Of these,

1. the power of concealment is destroyed by knowledge. By this the enlightened one does not attain another birth.
2. but by the power of *prārabdha* like the roasted seed, the power of projection (*avidyāleśa*) remains.

Q. 234: How is the world known in *jīvanmukti*?

Ans: 1. Just as by the knowledge of rope, the delusion of snake

---

[169] Individual in the form of body, bondage in the form of delusion, [are eliminated] removal in the form of liberation-while-living, all happen at once. This is the meaning.

[170] Like the stream (like river) flowing into the ocean-space.

[171] The modifying principle in the form of gross, subtle universes along with reflected consciousness.

is removed, later the result of delusion like shivering is known and

2. just as in the mirror the wise person knows the reflection and
3. just as in a dry land the wise person knows the mirage water,

the knower of reality in the state of *jīvanmukti* knows the sublated world.

Q. 235: What are the other examples for perception of a sublated world?

Ans: Example: In the Mahābhārata War, after the death of Droṇācārya, the fight continued with Aśvatthāmā and others. Then Kṛṣṇa took the resolve "may this chariot and the horses remain until the end of the war as it is". With this resolve he entered the battlefield. Aśvatthāmā wielded his *brahmāstra* (*agni astra*) and at that moment the chariot of Arjuna was reduced to ashes. Then also, by the strength of the resolve of Kṛṣṇa the charioteer, everything remained as it is. At the end of the war, there was a heap of ashes.

Explanation:

[1] The gross body is compared to the chariot.

[2] The two wheels are *puṇya* and *pāpa.*

[3] The flag is compared to three *guṇa*s.

[4] The reins are compared to five *prāṇa*s.

[5] The horses are compared to ten sense-organs.

[6] The path is in the form of sense objects of *śubha* and *aśubha.*

[7] The whip is the mind.

[8] The charioteer is intellect.

[9] The resolve is *prārabdha karma.*

[10] The seat is ego.

[11] The rider is *ātmā.*

[12] The weapons are compared to dispassion.

One who mounts on the chariot will enter into the battlefield of *satsaṅga.* One will receive the instruction of *mahāvākya* like *brahmāstra* from *guru* like Aśvatthāmā. By the rise of knowledge in the form of fire, it burns that very moment, the world consisting of body in the form of a chariot. Then also by the resolve of the intellect compared to Kr̥ṣṇa, whose resolve as *prārabdha karma* by its strength does not destroy the body and later also there is the cognition of the body.[172] This is known as *bādhita anuvr̥tti.*[173]

This is the example for cognition of world after sublation.

Q. 236: What is *videhamukti*?

Ans: 1. Remaining in the nature of *Brahman* without the perception of the world. Or

2. By the exhaustion of *prārabdha karma* ignorance, that is the cause for the modification in the form of later gross and subtle bodies, gets resolved into Consciousness. This is *videhamukti.*

Q. 237: By what means does the *avidyāleśa* with its effects resolve at the end of *prārabdha*?

---

[172] That which is subject to destruction is the counter-positive of destruction.

(1) The object of counter-positive of destruction is cognized and

(2) the object that is subject to sublation, its counter-positive cannot be cognized. But its non-existence in three periods of time is known. This is the difference between destruction and sublation.

[173] Just as the potter uses a stick to rotate the wheel, and even without using the stick the wheel rotates by its own for some time due to the speed, in the same way, even after sublation there is the cognition of the world with body and *prārabdha karma.* This is known as *bādhita anuvr̥tti.*

Ans: At the end of *prārabdha*, either in excessive or less state of unconsciousness (*mūrcchā*), even though there is the impossibility of *brahmākāra vṛtti*, and also the enlightened one is not bound by rules, then also, like in deep-sleep state, in that unconscious state also, there is the *saṁskāra* of *brahma-vidyā* as the thought, unto which the *avidyāleśa* resolves (gets destroyed). Just as the fire in a dry wood burns the grass and also the wood, the thought with *saṁskāra* destroys the world and also destroys itself (*saṁskāra* of knowledge). Later, the Unassociated, Pure, Existence, Consciousness, Absolute Peace, Self-luminous, Self-*Brahman* alone remains.

Thus ends the fourteenth digit of *Vicāracandrodaya* titled "Jīvanmukti and Videhamukti".

Kalā 15

The Object of Vedānta[174]

ललित छंद (*Lalita* Metre) (like in *Gopikāgīta*)

जन तु जानिले ज्ञेय अर्थकूं।
सकल छेद सं-दे अनर्थकूं।।

मुगति कौन है हेतु ताहिको।
जनक बीचको कौन वाहिको।। ३३ ।।

विषय बोधको कौन जानिले।
प्रतक ईशको तत्त्व मानिले।।

अहमअर्थकूं खूब सोजिले।
"तत" पदार्थकूं शुद्ध खोजिले।। ३४ ।।

परमआतमा एक मानिले।
तहँ सदादि ऐश्वर्य आनिले।।

सत चिदात्म सो सर्वदा अहै।
इस पीतांबरो ज्ञानकूं गहैं।। ३५ ।।

jana tu jānile jñeya arthakūṅ ।
sakala cheda saṁ-de anarthakūṅ ।।

---

174 (1) The true knowledge that arises from the valid source of knowledge, which is Vedānta, is called valid knowledge (*pramā*).

(2) The object arising from such a valid knowledge, which is worth knowing is called object of knowledge (*prameya*) which is described here. By the analysis of this digit (fifteenth), the doubt pertaining to the object of knowledge (*prameyagata saṁśaya*) gets removed. The description of doubt pertaining to the object of knowledge is elaborated [by Pitambar] in *Bālabodhinī Ṭīkā* of the text *Bālabodha* wherein nine instructions are discussed. One can refer to that work.

mugati kauna hai hetu tāhiko ।
janaka bīcako kauna vāhiko ।। 33 ।।

viṣaya bodhako kauna jānile ।
prataka īśako tattva mānile ।।

ahama arthakūṅ khūba sojile ।
"tata" padārthakūṅ śuddha khojile ।। 34 ।।

parama ātamā eka mānile ।
tahaṁ sadādi aiśvarya ānile ।।

sata cidātma so sarvadā ahai ।
isa pītāṁbaro jñānakūṅ gahai ।। 35 ।।

Know[175] the meaning of the "object",
uproot all doubts and evils.

What is the cause of liberation?
What arises in between[176] as the carrier? ।। 33 ।।

One who knows the object
accepts *Īśvara* distinctly as the truth
analyse the meaning of the word "I",[177]
ponder on the word-meaning of *tat* as pure ।। 34 ।।

Know the Supreme Self[178] as one,
then bring in the aspects like Existence etc.,
Existence Consciousness Self is always,[179]
this Pitambar's knowledge is firm ।। 35 ।।

Q. 238: What is the nature of liberation?

---

175 May the object of Vedānta be known.

176 Carrier (means to liberation, i.e. knowledge), in between arises (the intermediate means), what are they?

177 The meaning of I (*tvam*) word.

178 *Brahman*.

179 The nature of Existence, Consciousness, Absolute Happiness (the oneness of *Brahman–ātman*) is always (in three periods of time).

Ans: 1. Removal of bondage in the form of ignorance and its effects.

2. Attainment of absolute happiness *Brahman.*

This is the nature of liberation.

Q. 239: What is the direct means to liberation?

Ans: The direct knowledge of oneness of *Brahman* and *ātman.*

Q. 240: What is the indirect means to liberation?

Ans: *Niṣkāma karma,* meditation, etc. are the indirect means of liberation.

Q. 241: What is the content of this knowledge?

Ans: The oneness of *Brahman* and *ātman* is the content of this knowledge.

Q. 242: What is the nature of *ātmā*?

Ans: (1) That which is different from the body, sense-organ, vital air, mind, intellect, ignorance and nothingness, (2) Non-doer, (3) Non-enjoyer, (4) Unassociated, (5) All-pervasive, and (6) Consciousness are the nature of *ātmā.*

Q. 243: What is the nature of *Brahman*?

Ans: (1) Devoid of world, (2) Unassociated, (3) Complete, and (4) Consciousness are the nature of *Brahman.*

Q. 244: How is this oneness of *Brahman* and *ātmā*?

Ans: (1) Existence, Consciousness, Absolute Happiness; (2) Nature of overlordship; (3) Always present, these represent the oneness of *Brahman* and *ātmā.*

Q. 245: What is the nature of knowledge?

Ans: The conviction of non-difference of *jīva* and *Brahman* is the nature of knowledge.

Q. 246: What is the direct proximate means to knowledge?

Ans: *Śravaṇa* or listening directly from a *brahmaniṣṭha guru* the meaning of the *mahāvākya* is the direct proximate means to knowledge.

Q. 247: What is the indirect proximate means to knowledge?

Ans: (1) Discrimination, (2) dispassion, (3) sixfold mental disciplines (mastery of mind, sense-organ, study of one's own scripture, endurance, faith and concentration), (4) desire for liberation, (5) analysis of the word-meanings of *tat* and *tvam,* (6) *śravaṇa* [application of sixfold indicators to arrive at the central theme of Vedānta], (7) *manana,* and (8) *nididhyāsana* — these eight are the indirect proximate means to knowledge.

Q. 248: What are the remote means to knowledge?

Ans: *Niṣkāma karma, niṣkāma upāsanā,* etc. are the remote means to knowledge.

Q. 249: How many means are there to knowledge totally?

Ans: There are (more than) eleven means to knowledge totally.

Thus ends the fifteenth digit of *Vicāracandrodaya* titled "The Object of Vedānta".

Kalā 16

Concise Lexicon of Vedānta

ललित छंद (*Lalita* Metre)

निष्कलं निजं वेदहीं वदे।
षटदशं कला ब्रह्ममैं नदे।

निरवयेव जो निष्कलंक सो।
इकरसं सदा अंगता न सो।। ३६ ।।

हिरण्यगर्भ औ श्रद्धया नभो।
पवन तेज कं भूमि इंद्रिभो।

मन अनाज औ शक्ति सत्तपो।
करमलोक नामामनूजपो।। ३७ ।।

षटदशं कला एहि जानिले।
जडउपाधिको धर्म मानिले।

अनुगताश्रयोपुष्पसूत्रवत्।
निज चिदात्म पीतांबरो हि सत्।। ३८ ।।

niṣkalaṁ nijaṁ vedahīṁ vade।
ṣaṭadaśaṁ kalā brahmamaiṅ nade।

niravayeva jo niṣkalaṅka so।
ikarasaṁ sadā aṅgatā na so।। 36 ।।

hiraṇyagarbha au śraddhayā nabho।
pavana teja kaṁ bhūmi indribho।

mana anāja au śakti sattapo।
karamaloka nāmāmanūjapo।। 37 ।।

ṣaṭadaśaṁ kalā ehi jānile।
jaḍaupādhiko dharma mānile।

anugatāśrayopuṣpasūtravat।
nija cidātma pītāṁbaro hi sat।। 38 ।।

Divisionless is Self, so declares the Veda,
the sixteen parts are not in *Brahman*.

Partless is that which is divisionless,
is one essence always without parts || 36 ||

Hiraṇyagarbha and *śraddhā*, space,
air, fire, water, earth, sense-organs,
mind, food, power,[180] austerity,
action, worlds, name,[181] *mantra* || 37 ||

Know these to be the sixteen parts,
realize the adjunct matter as the entity.

Immanent is the substratum like the thread of a garland,
Self which is Consciousness is Existence, Pitambar || 38 ||

Advaitic Concepts in 2

Adhyātma-tāpa (2)

The present gross and subtle bodies with *ātmā* as the substratum is called *adhyātmā*. The sorrow in them is called *adhyātma-tāpa*.

1. *ādhi-tāpa* — is the sorrow at the mental level
2. *vyādhi-tāpa* — is the pain at the physical level

Adhyāsa (2)

The object of knowledge of delusion and the knowledge of delusion.

1. *Arthādhyāsa* — the object of knowledge of delusion like snake or body, world, etc.
2. *Jñānādhyāsa* — the knowledge of delusion (knowledge of snake or body, world, etc.)

---

180 Strength.

181 Recitation of *mantras*.

***Asambhāvanā* (2)**

Knowledge of the impossibility.

1. *Pramāṇagata asambhāvanā* — knowledge of the impossibility with regard to the means of knowledge (Veda).
2. *Prameyagata asambhāvanā* — knowledge of the impossibility with regard to the object of knowledge (the object of the means is liberation).

***Ahaṁkāra* (2)**

1. *Śuddha ahaṁkāra* — identification with one's own self.
2. *Aśuddha ahaṁkāra* — identification with non-self like body etc.

1. *Sāmānya ahaṁkāra* — free from the notion of the attribute like body etc., there is only the manifestation of "I".
2. *Viśeṣa ahaṁkāra* — where "I" manifests along with the attributes of the body, etc. (like name and class).

1. *Mukhya ahaṁkāra* — where "I" is identified with body etc., reflected consciousness and witness consciousness as one, and due to delusion the "I" is taken to be the combination of all these and referred to by the word "I". This is *mukhya ahaṁkāra* (the word "I" that is known by primary signification).
2. *Amukhya ahaṁkāra* — by discrimination [1] during empirical transaction there is body, etc., with the reflected consciousness [2] from the transcendental angle, there is only the unchanging principle which is the meaning of the word "I". This is *amukhya ahaṁkāra* (the word "I" that is known by secondary signification).

***Ajñāna* (2)**

1. *Samaṣṭi-ajñāna* — that which is the content of the macro

mind likened to a forest, or a genus, or a reservoir (lake).

2. *Vyaṣṭi-ajñāna* — that which is the content of a micro mind likened to a tree, a particular or a drop of water.

1. *Mūlājñāna* — the ignorance that conceals the Pure Consciousness.

2. *Tūlājñāna* — the ignorance that conceals the Consciousness conditioned by a pot, etc.

***Ajñāna-Śakti* (2)**

1. *Āvaraṇa śakti* — the power which conceals the substratum.
2. *Vikṣepa śakti* — the power which manifests the world and the world-knowledge.

***Upāsanā* (2)**

1. *Saguṇa upāsanā* — meditation on the causal *Brahman* (*Īśvara*) and effectual *Brahman* (e.g. *Hiraṇyagarbha*).
2. *Nirguṇa upāsanā* — meditation on Pure *Brahman*.

***Gandha* (2)**

1. *Sugandha* [good smell].
2. *Durgandha* [bad smell].

***Jāti* (2)**

That which pervades many things and itself has only one attribute.

1. *Para jāti* — "pot is" — this inhering existence is in all pots. This is referred to as *para* (superior) in the Nyāya system.
2. *Apara jāti* — that which is different from existence is pot-ness etc. and this class is referred to as *apara* (inferior) by the Nyāya system.

1. *Vyāpya jāti* — the genus which is inherent in the pervasive class (less pervasive) is called *vyāpya jāti*. Just as in the class of human beings is inherent (belonging to one place) the class of brāhmaṇa, kṣatriya, etc. These are less pervasive classes.
2. *Vyāpaka jāti* — that class which remains more pervasive than the *vyāpya jāti*. Just as the class of human is more pervasive than the class of brāhmaṇa. *Vyāpya* and *vyāpaka jāti*s are the divisions of *aparajāti*.

***Nigraha* (2)**

(1) *Krama nigraha* — where the mind is disciplined by following the order of *yama, niyama*, etc., of the eight-fold steps of Yoga is called discipline in order.

(2) *Haṭha nigraha* — where the mind is disciplined by restraining the *prāṇa* and taking to the practice of *mudrā* like *sāmbhavī* etc. is called discipline by *haṭha*.

***Niḥśreyasa* (2)**

1. *Anartha nivṛtti* [removal of sorrow].
2. *Paramānanda prāpti* [attainment of absolute happiness].

***Paramahaṁsa Saṁnyāsa* (2)**

1. *Vividiṣā saṁnyāsa* — renunciation with a desire to know, for the sake of attainment of knowledge.
2. *Vidvat saṁnyāsa* — after knowledge, taking to mendicant life for realization of "absolute peace" different from *jīvanmukti* that was attained through *vāsanā-kṣaya, manonāśa* and practice of *tattva-jñāna*. Such a renunciation is called *vidvat saṁnyāsa*.

***Prapañca* (2)**

1. *Bāhya prapañca* [external world of objects].
2. *Āntara prapañca* [internal world of thoughts].

Prajñā (2)

1. *Sthita prajñā* [firm knowledge].
2. *Asthita prajñā* [unfirm knowledge].

Lakṣaṇā (2)

1. *Svarūpa lakṣaṇā* — that differentiating characteristic which exists always.
2. *Taṭastha lakṣaṇā* — that differentiating characteristic that remains at times.

Vākya (2)

1. *Avāntara vākya* [the Vedic statements that reveal the nature of *jīvātmā* and *paramātmā*].
2. *Mahāvākya* [the Vedic statements that reveal the oneness of *jīvātmā* and *paramātmā*].

Vāda (2)

1. *Pratibimbavāda* [theory of reflection].
2. *Avacchedavāda* [theory of delimitation].

Viparīta bhāvanā (2)

1. *Pramāṇagata viparīta bhāvanā* [contradictory idea regarding to the means of knowledge].
2. *Prameyagata viparīta bhāvanā* [contradictory idea regarding to the object of knowledge].

Śabda (2)

1. *Varṇa-rūpa śabda* [word in the form of letters].
2. *Dhvani-rūpa śabda* [word in the form of suggestion].

Śabda-saṅgati (2)

1. *Śakti vṛtti* [primary power of words to convey a meaning].

2. *Lakṣaṇā vr̥tti* [secondary power of words to convey a meaning].

***Saṁpatti* (2)**

1. *Daivī sampatti* [qualities like fearlessness, purity of mind and charity].
2. *Āsurī sampatti* [qualities like pride, arrogance, greed and anger].

(*See *Bhagavad-Gītā,* chap. 16.)

***Saṁśaya* (2)**

1. *Pramāṇagata saṁśaya* [doubt with regard to the means of knowledge].
2. *Prameyagata saṁśaya* [doubt with regard to the object of knowledge].

***Samādhi* (2)**

1. *Savikalpa* [meditation in which the *tripuṭī* division remain].
2. *Nirvikalpa* [meditation in which the *tripuṭī* division resolve].

***Sūkṣma-śarīram* (2)**

1. *Samaṣṭi* [macro subtle body, *Hiraṇyagarbha*].
2. *Vyaṣṭi* [micro subtle body, *taijasa*].

***Sthūla-śarīram* (2)**

1. *Samaṣṭi* [macro gross body, *Virāṭ*].
2. *Vyaṣṭi* [micro gross body, *viśva*].

Advaitic Concepts in 3

***Adhyātmādi* (3)**

1. *Indriya* (*adhyātmā*) [the individual sense-organs].

2. *Devatā* (*adhidaiva*) [the respective presiding deities of sense-organs].
3. *Viṣaya* (*adhibhūta*) [the sense objects].

Antaḥkaraṇa doṣa **(3)**

[The defects in the mind.]

1. *Mala-doṣa* — the demerits accumulated in all past births.
2. *Vikṣepa-doṣa* — the mental disturbances.
3. *Āvaraṇa-doṣa* — ignorance of the nature [of Self].

Arthavāda **(3)**

A statement of eulogy or censure.

1. *Anuvāda* — the statement whose meaning can be proved by another means of knowledge, as in the example "fire is remover of cold".
2. *Guṇavāda* — that which is contradictory to other means of knowledge; but is meaningful by the attribute of the predicative word, as in the statement "the sacrifical post is sun", is meaningful by the attribute of brilliance of the predicative word "sun".
3. *Bhūtārthavāda* — is the valid means for its own meaning, and by secondary signification the predicative meaning is extolled, as in the statement "with *vajra* in hand is Purandara".

Avadhi **(Limit) (3)**

1. Knowledge limitation.
2. Dispassion limitation.
3. Mental mastery limitation.

Avasthā **(3)**

1. *Jāgrat avasthā* [waking state].

2. *Svapna avasthā* [dream state].
3. *Suṣupti avasthā* [deep-sleep state].

Ātmā **(3)**

1. *Jñānātmā* — intellect.
2. *Mahānātmā* — the *mahat* principle.
3. *Śāntātmā* — Pure *Brahman.*

Ātmabheda **(3)**

1. *Mithyātmā* — the gross and subtle bodies.
2. *Gauṇātmā* — son etc.
3. *Mukhyātmā* — witness consciousness (*kūṭastha*).

Ānanda **(3)**

1. *Brahmānanda* — the original *ānanda* obtained during *samādhi* or deep sleep state.
2. *Viṣayānanda* — on obtaining sense objects in waking and dream states, due to which the mind is single-pointed, in which for a moment the original *ānanda* gets reflected is called *viṣayānanada,* it is also known as *leśānanda* or *mātrānanda.*
3. *Vāsanānanda* — is the *ānanda* experienced on rise from deep sleep, or in a state of indifference.

Āndhyādi **(3)**

Blindness is the property of eyes. It indicates the property of other sense-organs like deafness and dumbness. The dullness and intelligence are in all the sense-organs.

1. *Āndhya* — non-grasp of sense objects through sense-organs like eyes.
2. *Māndya* — partial grasp of sense objects through the sense-organs.

3. *Paṭutva* — complete grasp of sense objects through the sense-organs.

***Uddeśādi* (3)**

1. *Uddeśya* — extol by name.
2. *Lakṣaṇa* — the special attribute (that which is present in one object only).
3. *Parīkṣā* — examination (enquiry into the defects like over-applicability etc.)

***Eṣaṇā* (*Desire or Impressions*) (3)**

1. *Putraiṣaṇā* — desire for son.
2. *Vittaiṣaṇā* — desire for wealth.
3. *Lokaiṣaṇā* — desire that everyone should praise me and none should criticize me, or the desire for higher worlds.

***Kartavyādi* (3)**

1. *Kartavya* — means of knowledge that ought to be done.
2. *Jñātavya* — object of knowledge that ought to be known (the oneness of *Brahman* and *ātman*).
3. *Prāptavya* — result of knowledge, liberation that is to be attained.

***Karma* (3)**

1. *Puṇya* [merits]
2. *Pāpa* [demerits]
3. *Miśra* [mixture of merits and demerits]

1. *Sañcita* — accumulated results of actions from countless past births.
2. *Āgāmī* — action performed in the current birth, whose results are yet to fructify.
3. *Prārabdha* — the fructified result of the current birth.

Karmādi (3)

1. *Karma* — actions prescribed in the Vedas.
2. *Vikarma* — actions prohibited by the Vedas.
3. *Akarma* — non-performance of the enjoined actions or [performance of the] prohibited actions of the Vedas.

Kāraṇa (3)

Means for action

1. *Mana* [mind].
2. *Vāṇī* [speech].
3. *Kāya* [body].

Kāraṇavāda (3)

1. *Ārambhavāda* — just as the old house of grandfather gets destroyed, from those collected bricks, again a new house is created, in the same way, on the destruction of earth, which are the effects, the causal atoms remain, from which another earth is born. This view of Nyāya School is known as *Ārambhavāda* in which there is the difference between effect and cause.
2. *Pariṇāmavāda* — just as milk modifies to become curd, according to the Sāṁkhyas, the *prakṛti* modifies to become the world. And according to the view of the meditators, *Brahman* modifies to become world and individual beings. Those who accept this theory of modification consider that effect and cause are non-different.
3. *Vivartavāda* — just as the unchanging substratum in the form of rope, becomes another entity "snake" of a different order of reality, that rope is said to be transfigurative (an imagined cause). In the unchanging *Brahman*, which is the substratum, another entity of different order of reality called world is superimposed.

That *Brahman* is transfigurative (imagined cause). This theory of transfiguration is accepted by Advaita Vedānta. Here also there is non-difference between effect and cause by the method of sublation.

Kāla **(3)**

1. *Bhūta kāla* [past time].
2. *Bhaviṣyat kāla* [future time].
3. *Vartamāna kāla* [present time].

Jāgrat **(3)**

1. *Jāgrat-jāgrat* — the present waking time which is directly witnessed.
2. *Jāgrat-svapna* — the mental world of thoughts pertaining to the past or future thought seen in the waking state.
3. *Jāgrat-suṣupti* — when the mind due to delusion is immobile in the waking state.

Jīva **(3)**

1. *Pāramārthika jīva* — the witness consciousness (unchanging).
2. *Vyāvahārika jīva* — individual with reflected consciousness in the internal organ.
3. *Prātibhāsika jīva* — in the *vyāvahārika jīva* is the superimposed *jīva* of the dream.

1. *Viśva* — the individual with an identification with the three bodies in waking state.
2. *Taijasa* — the individual with an identification with subtle and causal bodies, without the identity of gross body, during dream state.
3. *Prājña* — in deep-sleep, the identification with gross

and subtle bodies is given up and the identity with causal body remains.

***Tāpa* (3)**

Sorrow

1. *Adhyātma-tāpa* — the pain caused due to gross and subtle bodies, which are called *ādhi* and *vyādhi*, is called *adhyātma tāpa*.
2. *Adhidaiva-tāpa* — afflictions due to natural forces like cold, heat, excessive rain, lack of rain, fall of lightning and earthquake are known as *adhidaiva-tāpa*.
3. *Adhibhūta-tāpa* — sorrow caused by something perceptible other than one's own body, like fear of tiger, enemy and thief is called *adhibhūta-tāpa*.

***Nādādi* (3)**

1. *Nāda* — *oṁkāra* or quality of sound or the four kinds of speech known as *parā*.
2. *Bindu* — the *turīya* which is the unmanifest form of *oṁkāra*.
3. *Kalā* — the *akāra*, part of *oṁkāra*, of the nature of *parā* sound (parts of sound).

***Nivṛtti* (3)**

1. *Bhrama-nivṛtti* — removal of delusion of identity by destruction of confusion (non-discrimination) by knowledge.
2. *Sahaja-nivṛtti* — falsification by knowledge of the natural identity and its destruction after the fall of the body of the enlightened.
3. *Karmaja-nivṛtti* — the disappearance of identity with *karma* of an enlightened by the exhaustion of the fructified results.

Pāpa karma (3)

1. *Utkr̥ṣṭa pāpa karma* [severe unrighteous act].
2. *Madhyama pāpa karma* [mediocre unrighteous act].
3. *Sāmānya pāpa karma* [general unrighteous act].

Puṇya karma (3)

1. *Utkr̥ṣṭa puṇya karma* [superior righteous act].
2. *Madhyama puṇya karma* [mediocre righteous act].
3. *Sāmānya puṇya karma* [general righteous act].

Prapañca (3)

1. *Sthūla prapañca* [gross universe].
2. *Sūkṣma prapañca* [subtle universe].
3. *Kāraṇa prapañca* [causal universe].

Prāṇāyāma (3)

1. *Pūraka* [filling up the lungs with air, by deep inhalation].
2. *Kumbhaka* [retaining the air, by holding the breathe].
3. *Recaka* [releasing the air compelety, by exhalation].

Prārabdha (3)

1. *Icchā prārabdha* [fructified favourable results].
2. *Anicchā prārabdha* [fructified unfavourable results].
3. *Parecchā prārabdha* [fructified results favourable for others].

Brahma (3)

1. *Virāṭ* [macro gross universe].
2. *Hiraṇyagarbha* [macro subtle universe].
3. *Īśvara* [macro causal universe].

***Miśra karma* (3)**

1. *Utkṛṣṭa miśra karma* [intense mixed act].
2. *Madhyama miśra karma* [mediocre mixed act].
3. *Sāmānya miśra karma* [general mixed act].

***Mūrti* (3)**

1. Brahmā.
2. Viṣṇu.
3. Śiva.

***Lakṣaṇa doṣaḥ* (3)**

Defects of a definition

1. *Avyāpti doṣa* — the definition that gets applied to only one part of the definitum.
2. *Ativyāpti doṣa* — the over-applicability of the definition that includes other than the definitum.
3. *Asambhava doṣa* — the inapplicability of the definition in the definitum.

***Vādādi* (3)**

Discussion or disputation.

1. *Vāda* — dialogue between a teacher and the disciple, a discussion meant to arrive at the truth.
2. *Jalpa* — the opponent's argument with logical means of knowledge, skill and scholarliness, are refuted with the objective to establish one's own school of thought.
3. *Vitaṇḍā* — the argument of a fool without support of logic. Or, establishing one's own system through the refutation of other schools of thought. As done by Śrī Harṣa in his *khaṇḍaṇa* text.

Vidhi vākya **(3)**

1. *Apūrva vidhi* — the statement of injunction of an unknown action [in a context. For example, the statement "paddy is to be sprinkled" is an unknown action enjoined here].
2. *Niyama vidhi* — the statement of restriction of a known action. [For example, "paddy is to be pounded", to remove the husk. This is a known action, but here the action is restricted to only pounding as there are several methods of removing the husk.]
3. *Parisaṁkhyā vidhi* — the statement of permission. [It is not a compulsory act but a permission given as an option. Like "eat fruits during *ekādaśī* fast". It also indicates exclusion.]

Veda kāṇḍa **(3)**

1. *Karma-kāṇḍa.*
2. *Upāsanā-kāṇḍa.*
3. *Jñāna-kāṇḍa* [also known as Upaniṣad].

Śarīra **(3)**

1. *Sthūla* [gross body].
2. *Sūkṣma* [subtle body].
3. *Kāraṇa* [causal body].

Śravaṇādi **(3)**

1. *Śravaṇa* [listening to the Vedāntic scriptures from a *guru*].
2. *Manana* [analysis of the Vedāntic scriptures and removal of doubts].
3. *Nididhyāsana* [dedicated time for assimilation of the Vedāntic teaching].

***Śravaṇādi phala* (3)**

1. *Pramāṇa saṁśaya nāśa* — (result of *śravaṇa*) [removal of doubt related to the means of knowledge].
2. *Prameya saṁśaya nāśa* — (result of *manana*) [removal of doubt related to the object of knowledge].
3. *Viparyaya nāśa* — (result of *nididhyāsana*) [destruction of contradictory notions].

***Sambandha* (3)**

1. *Saṁyoga sambandha* [relation of association].
2. *Samavāya sambandha* [relation of inherence].
3. *Tādātmya sambandha* [relation of identity].

***Suṣupti* (3)**

1. *Suṣupti-jāgrat* — happiness due to *sāttvika* mental modification.
2. *Suṣupti-svapna* — sorrow due to *rājasika* mental modification.
3. *Suṣupti-suṣupti* — deep sleep due to *tāmasika* mental modification.

***Suṣuptyādi* (3)**

1. *Suṣupti* — deep sleep.
2. *Mūrcchā* — swoon.
3. *Samādhi* — deep contemplation.

***Svapna* (3)**

1. *Svapna-jāgrat* — seeing dream as object of reality.
2. *Svapna-svapna* — seeing rope as snake due to delusion.
3. *Svapna-suṣupti* — forgetting the experienced dream.

***Hetvādi* (3)**

1. *Hetu* [reason].
2. *Svarūpa* [nature].
3. *Phala* [result].

***Jñātādi* (3)**

1. *Jñātā* [knower].
2. *Jñāna* [knowledge].
3. *Jñeya* [object of knowledge].

***Jñāna pratibandhaka* (3)**

1. *Saṁśaya* [doubt].
2. *Asambhāvanā* [impossibility].
3. *Viparīta bhāvanā* [contradictory notion].

***Jñānādi* (3)**

1. *Jñāna* [self-knowledge].
2. *Vairāgya* [dispassion].
3. *Upaśama* [restrain].

Advaitic Concepts in 4

***Anubandha* (4)**

The fourfold factors that connect a seeker or reader to the text.

1. *Adhikārī* — an eligible seeker is one who has removed the defects of *mala* and *vikṣepa*, and acquired the fourfold qualities like discrimination etc.
2. *Viṣaya* — the subject matter of Vedānta Śāstra is the oneness of *Brahman* and *ātman*.
3. *Prayojana* — [benefit] destruction of all sorrows and attainment of absolute peace is liberation.

4. *Sambandha* — the relation of revealer–revealed between the text and the subject matter.

***Antaḥkaraṇa* (4)**

1. *Manas* — the thought of resolve and alternatives [indecisive, emotional faculty].
2. *Buddhi* — the thought of conviction [decisive, rational faculty].
3. *Cittam* — memory.
4. *Ahaṁkāra* — the thought of identity as "I".

***Ārtādi bhakta* (4)**

1. *Ārta* — one who is sorrowful due to the afflictions of *adhyātma* etc.
2. *Jijñāsu* — one with a desire to know the Truth.
3. *Arthārthī* — one with a desire to enjoy the benefits of this world and the other world.
4. *Jñānī* — the enlightened liberated one.

***Āśrama* (4)**

1. *Brahmacarya* [student life].
2. *Gṛhastha* [married life].
3. *Vānaprastha* [life of meditation].
4. *Saṁnyāsa* [mendicant life].

***Utpatyādi kriyā* (4)**

The result of action.

(1) *Utpatti* — origination, as the action of potter results in origination of a pot.

(2) *Prāpti* — action like movement resulting in reaching a desired destination.

(3) *Vikāra* — attainment of another form. As by the action

of cooking (in the kitchen) the result of action is change of food (stirring).

(4) *Saṁskāra* — (1) removal of impurity, and (2) attainment of purity. In this way, purification is of two kinds: (1) just as by the action of washing clothes, the dirt is removed, and (2) by the action of dipping the cloth in saffron, there is the result of cloth acquiring red colour.

Citta-nirodha-yukti **(4)**

1. *Adhyātma vidyā* [knowledge of self].
2. *Sādhu saṅga* [association with noble ones].
3. *Vāsanā tyāga* [eliminating ignoble impressions].
4. *Prāṇāyāma* [control of breathing movement].

Dharmādi **(4 *Puruṣārtha*)**

1. *Dharma* — the merits through either *sakāma* or *niṣkāma karma*.
2. *Artha* — the means for attainment of happiness in this world and the other world.
3. *Kāma* — enjoyments of this world and the other world.
4. *Mokṣa* — removal of sorrow and attainment of peace.

Puruṣārtha **(4)** [See above *Dharmādi*.]

Pramāṇa **(4)**

The instrument of knowledge is means of knowledge. Here, the four types enumerated are based on Nyāya system.

1. *Pratyakṣa* [perception].
2. *Anumāna* [inference].
3. *Upamāna* [comparison].
4. *Śabda* [testimony].

Brahmavidādi (4)

1. *Brahmavit* — the enlightened one elevated to the fourth *bhūmikā*.
2. *Brahmavidvara* — the enlightened one elevated to the fifth *bhūmikā*.
3. *Brahmavidvarīyān* — the enlightened one elevated to the sixth *bhūmikā*.
4. *Brahmavidvariṣṭha* — the enlightened one elevated to the seventh *bhūmikā*.

Bhūtagrāma (4)

1. *Jarāyuja* — human, animal, etc. [born of womb].
2. *Aṇḍaja* — birds, snake, etc. [born from eggs].
3. *Udbhija* — trees [sprouts, breaking open the earth].
4. *Svedaja* — lice, mosquito, etc. [born due to moisture].

Maitryādi (4)

1. *Maitrī* — being friendly with a wealthy person, or like-minded ones, or devotee of god, or ritualist-meditators.
2. *Karuṇā* — compassionate towards those with afflictions, or with inferior qualities, or ignorant ones, or desirers of knowledge.
3. *Muditā* — love towards those with merits, or with noble qualities, or god, or liberated one.
4. *Upekṣā* — indifferent, without like or dislike towards sinners, unrighteous ones, enemy and commoner.

Mokṣa dvārapāla (4)

Gateways to liberation.

1. *Śama* [mastery of mind].
2. *Santoṣa* [contentment].

3. *Vicāra* [enquiry (discrimination)].
4. *Satsaṅga* [noble association].

***Yoga bhūmikā* (4)**

1. *Vāṇī laya* [resolution of speech].
2. *Mano-laya* [serenity of mind].
3. *Buddhi laya* [resolution of intellect].
4. *Ahaṁkāra laya* [falsification of ego].

***Varṇa* (4)**

1. Brāhmaṇa
2. Kṣatriya
3. Vaiśya
4. Śūdra

***Vartamāna jñāna pratibandha nivṛtti hetu* (4)**

The cause for the removal of obstacles to knowledge pertaining to the present time.

1. *Śamādi* — is the remover of power of attraction towards sense objects.
2. *Śravaṇa* — is the remover of sluggishness in the intellect.
3. *Manana* — is the remover of dry-logic.
4. *Nididhyāsana* — is the remover of habitual notions.

***Vartamāna jñāna pratibandha* (4)**

Obstacles to knowledge at the present time.

1. *Viṣayāśakti* — passionate towards sense objects.
2. *Buddhi māndyam* — dullness of the intellect.
3. *Kutarka* — dry-logic.
4. *Durāgraha* — habitual notions.

***Vivekādi* (4)**

1. *Viveka* [power of discrimination].
2. *Vairāgya* [dispassion].
3. *Ṣaṭ-sampatti* [sixfold mental disciplines: mastery of the mind, mastery of the sense-organs, performance of one's own prescribed duty, endurance, faith in scriptures and *guru,* and single-pointed concentration].
4. *Mumukṣutā* [desire for liberation].

***Śabda-pravṛtti-nimitta* (4)**

1. *Jāti* [genus, universal, class].
2. *Guṇa* [attribute].
3. *Kriyā* [action].
4. *Sambandha* [relation].

***Saṁnyāsa* (4)**

1. *Kuṭīcaka* [a renunciate who stays in one place].
2. *Bahūdaka* [a renunciate who wanders].
3. *Haṁsa* [a renunciate with intense dispassion].
4. *Paramahaṁsa* [a renunciate who takes to the direct means of liberation].

***Samādhi vighna* (4)**

Obstacles to meditation.

1. *Laya* [sleep].
2. *Vikṣepa* [distraction].
3. *Kaṣāya* [dullness].
4. *Rasāsvāda* [tasting the tranquillity].

***Sādhana catuṣṭaya sampatti* (4)**
(*see under Vivekādi*)

Sparśa **(4)**

1. *Śīta* [cold].
2. *Uṣṇa* [heat].
3. *Komala* [soft].
4. *Kaṭhina* [hard].

Advaitic Concepts in 5

Abhāva **(5)**

Content of non-apprehension.

1. *Prāgābhāva* — the effect that is non-existent before its origination.
2. *Pradhvaṁsābhāva* — the non-existence of effect after its destruction.
3. *Anyonyābhāva* — the mutual non-existence, as difference in colours, non-existence of pot in cloth and cloth in pot and so on.
4. *Atyantābhāva* — non-existence in three periods of time like non-existence of colour in air.
5. *Sāmayikābhāva* — temporal non-existence, like absence of pot on the ground.

Ajñāna bheda **(5)**

The different views of Advaita *ācārya*s regarding the concept of *ajñāna.*

1. *Māyā-avidyā-rūpa-ajñāna* — according to some (Svāmi Vidyāraṇya) *ajñāna* is of the nature of *māyā* (the macro-ignorance which is the adjunct of *Īśvara*) and *avidyā* (micro-ignorance which is the adjunct of *jīva*).
2. *Jñāna-kriyā-śakti-rūpa-ajñāna* — some state *ajñāna* as power to know and power to act.

3. *Vikṣepa-āvaraṇa-rūpa-ajñāna* — some state ignorance as the power of concealment and power of projection.
4. *Samaṣṭi-vyaṣṭi-rūpa-ajñāna* — some state ignorance is macro (adjunct of *Īśvara*) and micro (adjunct of *jīva*).
5. *Kāraṇa-rūpa ajñāna* — some state ignorance as the material cause of the world, which is the primordial matter that is the adjunct of *Īśvara*. In this view, the effect (internal sense-organ) with an adjunct is *jīva*.

***Upavāyu* (5)**

1. *Nāga* — air that is cause for vomiting or eructation.
2. *Kūrma* — air that is the cause for the function of opening and closing of eyes.
3. *Kṛkala* — air that functions during sneeze.
4. *Devadatta* — air that produces yawning.
5. *Dhanañjaya* — air that nourishes the body.

***Karma* (5)**

1. *Nitya karma* — the compulsory daily duties enjoined in the Vedas (bathing, *sandhyāvandana,* etc.).
2. *Naimittika karma* — the compulsory occasional duties enjoined (like *śrāddhā*).
3. *Kāmya karma* — actions enjoined for fulfilment of a particular desire (special rituals).
4. *Prāyaścitta karma* — the actions enjoined for removal of special sin that one may incur.
5. *Niṣiddha karma* — the prohibited actions (like the killing of a brāhmaṇa).

***Karmendriya* (5)**

1. *Vāk* [sense-organ of speech].
2. *Pāṇi* [sense-organ of grasping].

3. *Pāda* [sense-organ of locomotion].
4. *Upastha* [sense-organ of reproduction].
5. *Guda* [sense-organ of excretion].

Kośa **(5)**

1. *Annamaya kośa* [gross body]
2. *Prāṇamaya kośa* [subtle body, vital airs and sense-organs of action].
3. *Manomaya kośa* [subtle body, mind and sense-organs of knowledge].
4. *Vijñānamaya kośa* [subtle body, intellect and sense-organs of knowledge].
5. *Ānandamaya kośa* [causal body].

Kleśa **(5)**

1. *Avidyā*

   [1] notion of happiness in lieu of sorrow

   [2] notion of self in the non-self

   [3] notion of eternity in the non-eternal

   [4] notion of purity in the impure.

   These four kinds of effect are due to ignorance.
2. *Asmitā* — the idea of oneness of witness (self) and mind (general I-ness).
3. *Rāga* — firm attachment (love for progress).
4. *Dveṣa* — anger.
5. *Abhiniveṣa* — fear of death.

Khyāti **(5)**

The mechanism of cognition and its expression.

1. *Asat-khyāti* — Śūnyavādins. The cognition of non-existent "snake" (without nature) in rope is considered as real.

2. *Ātma-khyāti* — Kṣaṇikavijñānavādins. Self of the nature of momentariness is cognized as "snake".

3. *Anyathā-khyāti* — Naiyāyikas. The cognition of "snake" that is in a distant place, on rope, due to the strength of defect. Otherwise, the object of knowledge which is rope is mistaken as knowledge of "snake".

4. *Akhyāti-khyāti* — Sāṁkhya-Prābhākara. In the statement, "this is snake" — "this" part refers to the rope which is the object of perceptual cognition and "snake" part refers to the memory of past experienced snake. They are two different forms of knowledge. Due to the strength of defect, there is non discrimination (non-apprehension of the difference).

5. *Anirvacanīya-khyāti* — Advaita Siddhānta. Due to ignorance, in the rope, the indescribable (different from *sat* and *asat*) snake is cognized and known.

***Jīvanmukti prayojana* (5)**

Even though liberation while living is an attained one for an enlightened person, here the word *jīvanmukti* refers to the state of happiness different from *jīvanmukti* (the fifth *bhūmikā* onwards). The benefit of this is fivefold.

1. *Jñāna rakṣā* — even though, once attained firm knowledge cannot be destroyed, and knowledge need not be protected, then also, here the incessant mode of *Brahman*-thought is meant by the words "protection of knowledge".

2. *Tapa* — oneness of mind and sense-organs, or integration of body, speech and mind.

3. *Visaṁvāda abhāva* — absence of *jalpa* and *vitaṇḍāvāda.*

4. *Duḥkha-nivṛtti* — removal of seen (perceived) sorrow.

5. *Sukha prāpti* — attainment of happiness different from

unconcealed infinite and liberation which is one's own nature.

***Dṛṣṭānta* (5)**

The examples cited to show the falsity of the world.

1. Shell–silver.
2. Rope–snake.
3. Pillar–man.
4. Dryland and mirage-water — the reflection of the rays of the sun formed on the dry land (desert land) at noon-time is known as the mirage, in which there is the appearance of water and that is known as mirage-water.
5. Cloud-city.

***Niyama* (5)**

1. *Śauca* [physical purity].
2. *Santoṣa* [contentment].
3. *Tapa* [austerity].
4. *Svādhyāya* — regular study of one's own Vedic branch or study of *Gītā* etc.
5. *Īśvara praṇidhāna* — meditation on Lord in the form of *oṁkāra* etc.

***Pralaya* (5)**

1. *Nitya pralaya* — that which gets destroyed every moment like flame of a lamp or deep sleep.
2. *Naimittika pralaya* — that which is instrumental for the night of Brahmā or destruction of *bhūloka* and the three worlds downward.
3. *Dina pralaya* — the destruction of fourteen *manvantaras* that form the day of Brahmā. It is also known as

avāntara pralaya or *manvantara pralaya*. Some consider this as *naimittika pralaya*.

4. *Mahā pralaya* — the resolution of Brahmā along with space and all other elements at the end of 100 years of Brahmā.
5. *Ātyantika pralaya* — the negation of the entire world along with its cause by an enlightened one (absolute elimination).

***Prāṇādi* (5)**

1. *Prāṇa* [respiration].
2. *Apāna* [evacuation or rejection].
3. *Vyāna* [circulation].
4. *Udāna* [reaction, reversal].
5. *Samāna* [assimilation or digestion].

***Bheda* (5)**

1. Difference between *jīva* and *Īśvara.*
2. Difference between *jīva* and *jīva.*
3. Difference between *jīva* and *jaḍa* [matter].
4. Difference between *Īśvara* and *jaḍa.*
5. Difference between *jaḍa* and *jaḍa.*

***Bhrama* (5)**

(See Digit 6 [Q. 128].)

1. *Bheda bhrama* [delusion of difference].
2. *Kartṛ bhrama* [delusion of doership].
3. *Saṅga bhrama* [delusion of association].
4. *Vikāra bhrama* [delusion of modification].
5. *Satyatva bhrama* [delusion of reality of the world].

***Bhrama nivartaka dṛṣṭānta* (5)**

Examples to show the removal of delusions [see Q. 129].

1. Original-reflection
2. Red-crystal.
3. Pot-space.
4. Rope-snake.
5. Gold-ornament.

***Mahāyajña* (5)**

1. *Deva* [worship of gods].
2. *Ṛṣi* [reverence to sages by study of one's own scriptures].
3. *Pitṛ* [remembrance of ancestors].
4. *Manuṣya* [service to humanity].
5. *Bhūta* [protection of plants and animals].

***Yama* (5)**

1. *Ahiṁsā* [non-violence].
2. *Satya* [truthfulness].
3. *Brahmacarya* [celibacy].
4. *Aparigraha* — refrain from possessing more than what is necessary.
5. *Asteya* — non-stealing.

***Yoga bhūmikā* (5)**

1. *Kṣepa* — imbalance of the mind due to attachment, hatred, etc.
2. *Vikṣepa* — inability to concentrate during meditation due to extrovertedness.
3. *Mūḍha* — dullness due to sleep, tiredness, etc.

4. *Ekāgra* — concentration.
5. *Nirodha* — control.

Vacanādi (5)

1. *Vacana* [speech].
2. *Ādāna* [taking].
3. *Gamana* [movement].
4. *Rati* [pleasure].
5. *Mala-tyāga* [removal of impurity].

Śabdādi (5)

1. *Śabda* [sound].
2. *Sparśa* [touch].
3. *Rūpa* [form].
4. *Rasa* [taste].
5. *Gandha* [smell].

Sthūla bhūta (5)

Gross elements

1. *Ākāśa* — space.
2. *Vāyu* — air.
3. *Teja* — fire.
4. *Jala* — water.
5. *Pṛthvī* — earth.

Hetvābhāsa (5)

That which deviates from the definition of *hetu* [middle term], is defective *hetu*.

1. *Savyabhicāra* — [straying reason] the reason [knowability] which is present in a place [lake] where there is the absence of the thing to be proved is called

savyabhicāra. The argument here is "hill is fiery because it is knowable", here knowability exists in the lake also where there is the absence of fire. This is also known as *anaikāntika hetu*.

2. *Viruddha* — [self-contradicting reason] is that which is pervaded by the negation of the thing to be proved. In the argument, "sound is eternal because it is produced", here, producibility is pervasive of non-eternality which is of the nature of the negation of eternality. That which is produced is non-eternal, like a pot.
3. *Satpratipakṣa* — [antithetical reason] is that of which there exists another reason capable of proving the negation of the thing to be proved. In the argument, sound is eternal, because it is audible, like soundness; and sound is non-eternal because it is a product like a pot.
4. *Asiddha* — [unestablished reason] in respect of itself, is found in the argument "sound is a quality because it is visible", here visibility does not exist in sound, as audibility exists in sound only.
5. *Bādhita* — [contradicted reason] is one where the negation of the thing to be proved is established by another proof, e.g. fire is not hot because it is a substance like water. Here, the non-hotness is the thing to be proved. But hotness which is the negation of non-hotness is cognized through the sense-organ of skin, therefore, the above reason is known as contradicted reason.

***Jñānendriya* (5)**

Sense-organ of knowledge.

1. *Śrotra* [sense-organ of hearing].
2. *Tvak* [sense-organ of touch].
3. *Cakṣu* [sense-organ of sight].

4. *Jihvā* [sense-organ of taste].
5. *Ghrāṇa* [sense-organ of smell].

Advaitic Concepts in 6

Ajihvādi (6)

This is the characteristic feature of a renunciate.

1. *Ajihvatva* — free from the attachment of sense object.
2. *Napuṁsakatva* — vision of sameness in case of youth — girl or boy (sixteen years of age) and aged women.
3. *Paṁgutva* — not moving in a day more than what is required.
4. *Andhatva* — not seeing more than what is required, like while aiming a target with a bow.
5. *Badhiratva* — non-hearing of purposeless speech.
6. *Mugdhatva* — reduction of transaction.

Anādi padārtha (6)

That which is without origination.

1. *Jīva* — the individual self.
2. *Īśa* — the total self.
3. *Śuddha cetana* — Pure Consciousness.
4. *Avidyā* — ignorance.
5. *Cetana avidyā sambandha* — relationship between Consciousness and ignorance.
6. *Bheda* — the difference between Consciousness and ignorance.

Arivarga (6)

That which is opposed to the [attainment of] higher world; the group of enemies within (remaining inside).

1. *Kāma* — desire for enjoyment of the attained object.
2. *Krodha* — hatred.
3. *Lobha* — desire for attainment of the non-attained object.
4. *Moha* — non-discrimination of self and non-self or effect and cause.
5. *Mada* — pride (ego).
6. *Matsara* — intolerance of another's prosperity.

***Avasthā* (6)**

The stages of the gross body.

1. *Śiśu* — the physical body's one year duration.
2. *Kaumāra* — five-year age of the gross body.
3. *Pauganḍa* — the time period between six to ten years.
4. *Kiśora* — the age between eleven to fifteen.
5. *Yauvana* — the age between sixteen to forty.
6. *Jarā* — forty and above.

***Īśvara-bhaga* (6)**

1. *Samagra aiśvarya* [complete overlordship].
2. *Samagra dharma* [total righteousness].
3. *Samagra yaśa* [total fame].
4. *Samagra śrī* [complete prosperity].
5. *Samagra jñāna* [complete knowledge].
6. *Samagra vairāgya* [total dispassion].

***Īśvara jñāna* (6)**

1. *Utpatti–pralaya* [knowledge of origination and dissolution].
2. *Gati* [knowledge of movement of the individual beings].

3. *Āgati* [knowledge of the arrival of beings to this world].
4. *Vidyā* [self-knowledge].
5. *Avidyā* [primal matter].
6. *Vairāgya* [total dispassion].

***Ūrmi* (6)**

Ocean with waves in the form of bondage.

1. *Janma* [birth].
2. *Maraṇa* [death].
3. *Kṣudhā* [hunger].
4. *Tṛṣā* [thirst].
5. *Harṣa* [delight].
6. *Śoka* [sorrow].

Karma (6)

Regular duties.

1. *Snāna* [bathing].
2. *Japa* [repetition of lord's name].
3. *Homa* [sacrificial rites].
4. *Arcana* [worship of god].
5. *Ātithya* — sharing of food on arrival of an unknown person at the time of eating.
6. *Vaiśvadeva* — fire-ritual by offering oblations.

***Kauśika* (6)**

Constituents of the gross body.

1. *Tvak* [skin].
2. *Māṁsa* [flesh].
3. *Rudhira* [blood].
4. *Meda* [fat].

5. *Majjā* [marrow].
6. *Asthi* [bone].

***Pramāṇa* (6)**

1. *Pratyakṣa pramāṇa* — means for perceptual cognition is perception. The five sense-organs of knowledge like the sense-organ of hearing etc.
2. *Anumāna pramāṇa* — the means which is the knowledge of reason for inferential cognition. Like the knowledge of fire in hill by the knowledge of the reason which is smoke.
3. *Upamāna pramāṇa* — the knowledge of similarity is the means for comparison. Like in bison there is the knowledge of similarity of cow.
4. *Śabda pramāṇa* — instrument for valid testimony is the worldly and scriptural words.
5. *Arthāpatti pramāṇa* — the means for presumption is the knowledge of an explanatory fact. Like a "fat person does not eat during day" is presumed to eat during nights where "fatness" is the explanatory fact for presumption.
6. *Anupalabdhi pramāṇa* — the means for non-apprehension where there is the knowledge of the absence of a thing. Like, for the knowledge of the absence of pot on the ground, the means is non-cognition of pot.

***Bhrama* (6)**

1. *Kula.*
2. *Gotra.*
3. *Jāti.*
4. *Varṇa.*

5. *Āśrama.*
6. *Nāma.*

***Rasa* (6)**

Tastes

1. *Madhura* [sweet].
2. *Āmla* [acid].
3. *Lavaṇa* [saline].
4. *Kaṭuka* [pungent].
5. *Kaṣāya* [astringent].
6. *Tikta* [bitter].

***Liṅga* (6)**

The clues that are used for arriving at the core content of the Vedic statements.

1. *Upakrama-upasaṁhāra* — the sameness of introduction and conclusion.
2. *Abhyāsa* — repetition.
3. *Apūrvatā* — uniqueness.
4. *Phala* — result.
5. *Arthavāda* — eulogy [or censure].
6. *Upapatti* — proving example.

***Vikāra* (6)**

1. *Janma* [birth].
2. *Asti* — existence of a prior non-existent thing.
3. *Buddhi* — mature.
4. *Vipariṇāma* — change.
5. *Apakṣaya* — decline.
6. *Vināśa* — death.

***Vedāṅga* (6)**

1. *Śikṣā* [science of phonetics].
2. *Kalpa* [ritualistic procedure].
3. *Vyākaraṇa* [grammar].
4. *Nirukta* [etymology].
5. *Chanda* [prosody].
6. *Jyotiṣa* [astronomy and astrology].

***Śamādi* (6)**

1. *Śama* [mind control].
2. *Dama* [sensory control].
3. *Uparati* [balance of restrained mind].
4. *Titikṣā* [endurance].
5. *Śraddhā* [faith in Vedas and words of *guru*].
6. *Samādhāna* [concentration].

***Śāstra* (6)**

1. Sāṁkhya.
2. Yoga.
3. Nyāya.
4. Vaiśeṣika.
5. Pūrva-Mīmāṁsā.
6. Uttara-Mīmāṁsā.

***Samādhi* (6)**

1. *Bāhya-dṛśya-anuviddha* [withdrawal from external objects].
2. *Āntara-dṛśya-anuviddha* [withdrawal from internal thoughts].
3. *Bāhya-śabda-anuviddha* [withdrawal from external sound].

4. *Āntara-śabda-anuviddha* [withdrawal from internal sound].
5. *Bāhya-nirvikalpa* [withdrawal from external divisions].
6. *Āntara-nirvikalpa* [withdrawal from internal divisions].

***Sūtra* (6)**

1. *Jaimini-Sūtra.*
2. *Āśvalāyana-Sūtra.*
3. *Āpastamba-Sūtra.*
4. *Baudhāyana-Sūtra.*
5. *Kātyāyana-Sūtra.*
6. *Vaikhānasīya-Sūtra.*

Advaitic Concepts in 7

***Atalādi* (7)**

Worlds below earth.

1. *Atala.*
2. *Vitala.*
3. *Sutala.*
4. *Talātala.*
5. *Rasātala.*
6. *Mahātala.*
7. *Pātāla.*

***Avasthā* (7)**

Three states from the standpoint of reflected consciousness and four conditions that are causes for liberation.

1. *Ajñāna* — the indescribable beginningless positive entity with the powers of concealment and projection that is cause for the expression like "I don't know".

2. *Āvaraṇa* — the effect of ignorance which results in expressions like "does not exist" and "does not illumine".
3. *Vikṣepa* — world, body, etc. and their features along with their knowledge.
4. *Parokṣa jñāna* [indirect knowledge].
5. *Aparokṣa jñāna* [direct knowledge].
6. *Śokanāśa* — destruction of projection [elimination of delusion].
7. *Tṛpti* — contentment born out of knowledge.

Cetana (7)

1. *Īśvara cetana* — Consciousness conditioned by *māyā.*
2. *Jīva cetana* — Consciousness conditioned by *avidyā.*
3. *Śuddha cetana* — Consciousness without conditioning factor.
4. *Pramātā cetana* — Consciousness conditioned by internal organ.
5. *Pramāṇa cetana* — the thought which goes out through the sense-organs, reaches the place of sense object, and modifies is *pramāṇa*, and the consciousness conditioned by it is *pramāṇa cetana.*
6. *Prameya cetana* — the Consciousness conditioned by objects like pot (is differentiated from other objects).
7. *Pramā cetana* — the thought-modification in the form of "pot" is *pramā* which conditions Consciousness. It is also the reflected consciousness referred to as *pramiti cetana* or *phala cetana.*

Dravyādi padārtha (7)

The sevenfold classification of categories according to Nyāya system.

1. *Dravya* — the nine substances (that are the substratum of quality) are [1] earth, [2] water, [3] fire, [4] air, [5] space, [6] time, [7] direction, [8] Self, and [9] mind.
2. *Guṇa* — there are twenty-four qualities beginning from colour to impressions.
3. *Karma* — five kinds of movement are [1] upward, [2] downward, [3] contraction, [4] expansion, and [5] motion.
4. *Sāmānya* — *para* (existence) and *apara* (like pot-ness) are two kinds of genus.
5. *Samavāya* — that which is accepted in Vedānta as *tādātmya sambandha* [relation of identity] is considered in Nyāya system as special relation (eternal relation).
6. *Abhāva* — [1] prior non-existence, [2] posterior non-existence, [3] mutual non-existence, [4] absolute non-existence, and [5] temporal non-existence. These five types are in the form of the knowledge of non-existence of an object.
7. *Viśeṣa* — in Nyāya system, particularities are innumerable, ranging from medium-sized atoms.

***Dhātu* (7)**

1. *Rasa* — subtle (merits, demerits), middle (essence of food) and gross (impurity) are the threefold aspects of consumed food. Here, it refers to the middle part.
2. *Rudhira* [blood].
3. *Māṁsa* — flesh.
4. *Meda* — white flesh, fat.
5. *Majjā* — the bone-marrow.
6. *Asthi* [bone].
7. *Reta* [male-seed].

***Bhūrādi loka* (7)**

1. *Bhūloka.*
2. *Bhuvarloka.*
3. *Svarloka.*
4. *Maharloka.*
5. *Janaloka.*
6. *Tapoloka.*
7. *Satyaloka.*

***Maunādi* (7)**

1. *Mauna* [silence].
2. *Yogāsana* [posture].
3. *Yoga* [disciplines].
4. *Titikṣā* [endurance].
5. *Ekāntaśīlatā* [seclusion].
6. *Niḥspṛhatā* [unattachement].
7. *Samatā* [equanimity].

***Rūpa* (7)**

1. *Śukla* [white].
2. *Kṛṣṇa* [black].
3. *Pīta* [yellow].
4. *Rakta* [red].
5. *Harita* [green].
6. *Kapiśa* [brown].
7. *Citra* [variegated].

***Vyasana* (7)**

Those to be cast off.

1. Body.

2. Mind.
3. Anger.
4. Sense object.
5. Wealth.
6. Kingdom.
7. Servants.

***Jñāna-bhūmikā* (7)**
(See Digit 13, Q. 223.)

1. *Śubha icchā.*
2. *Suvicāraṇa.*
3. *Tanumānasā.*
4. *Sattvāpatti.*
5. *Asaṁsakti.*
6. *Padārthābhāvinī.*
7. *Turīyagā.*

Advaitic Concepts in 8

***Pāśa* (8)**
Binding factors.

1. *Dayā* [pity].
2. *Śaṅkā* [doubt].
3. *Bhaya* [fear].
4. *Lajjā* [shame].
5. *Nindā* [censure].
6. *Kula* [lineage].
7. *Śīla* [virtues].
8. *Dhana* [wealth].

***Purī* (8)**

1. Five sense-organs of knowledge.
2. Five sense-organs of action.
3. Four functions of internal organ.
4. Five vital airs.
5. Five elements.
6. Desire.
7. Three kinds of *karma.*
8. Impressions.

***Prakṛti* (8)**

1. Earth.
2. Water.
3. Fire.
4. Air.
5. Space.
6. Mind — macro mind with total identification.
7. Intellect — macro intellect which is the *mahat* principle.
8. I-identity — primal matter which is the causal ignorance, pure-ego, prior to the principle of *mahat.*

***Brahmacarya aṅga* (8)**

Without the following eight association.

1. Seeing a woman.
2. Touch.
3. Dice-game etc.
4. Praise.
5. Secret-talk.
6. Worry (remembrance).

7. Certainty.
8. Giving up of all the above.

***Mada* (8)**

1. *Kula mada* [pride of lineage].
2. *Śīla mada* [pride in virtues].
3. *Dhana mada* [pride in wealth].
4. *Rūpa mada* [pride in personality].
5. *Yauvana mada* [pride in youth].
6. *Vidyā mada* [pride in knowledge].
7. *Tapa mada* [pride in austerity].
8. *Rājya mada* [pride in prosperity].

***Mūrti mada* (8)**

1. *Pṛthvī mada* — identification with products of earth like bone and flesh.
2. *Jala mada* — identification with products of water like male-seed and female-seed.
3. *Teja mada* — identification with products of fire like hunger.
4. *Pavana mada* — identification with principles of air like movement (going abroad) and running.
5. *Ākāśa mada* — identification with principles of space like desire and anger.
6. *Candra mada* — bound with quality of moon like coolness.
7. *Sūrya mada* — bound with quality of sun like heat (anger).
8. *Ātma mada* — identification with knowledge, wealth, lineage, etc.

***Śabda śakti grahaṇa hetu* (8)**

Means for comprehending the meaning of words.

1. *Vyākaraṇa* [grammar].
2. *Upamāna* [comparison].
3. *Kośa* [lexicon].
4. *Āptavākya* [learned person].
5. *Vṛddhavyavahāra* [verbal usage].
6. *Vākya kośa* [complement-conclusion].
7. *Vivaraṇa* [explanation].
8. *Sannidhi* [contextual meaning].

***Samādhi aṅga* (8)**

1. *Yama* [disciplines].
2. *Niyama* [disciplines].
3. *Āsana* [posture].
4. *Prāṇāyāma* [breathing techniques].
5. *Pratyāhāra* [control].
6. *Dhāraṇa* [retention].
7. *Dhyāna* [meditation].
8. *Samādhi* [contemplation].

Advaitic Concepts in 9

***Tattva* (9)**

According to some school of thought, the subtle body consists of nine constituents.

1. *Śrotra* [sense-organ of hearing].
2. *Tvak* [sense-organ of touch].
3. *Cakṣu* [sense-organ of sight].
4. *Jihvā* [sense-organ of taste].

5. *Ghrāṇa* [sense-organ of smell].
6. *Mana* [mind].
7. *Buddhi* [intellect].
8. *Citta* [memory].
9. *Ahaṁkāra* [ego].

***Saṁsāra* (9)**

1. *Jñātā* [knower].
2. *Jñāna* [knowledge].
3. *Jñeya* [object of knowledge].
4. *Bhoktā* [reaper].
5. *Bhogya* [object of experience].
6. *Bhoga* [experience].
7. *Kartā* [doer].
8. *Karaṇa* [instrument].
9. *Kriyā* [action].

Advaitic Concepts in 10

***Nāḍikā-devatās* (10)**

1. *Iḍā* (*candra*) — in left nostril. Hari *devatā*.
2. *Piṅgalā* (*sūrya*) — in right nostril. Brahmā *devatā*.
3. *Suṣumṇā* (*madhyamā*) — centre of the nose. Rudra *devatā*.
4. *Gāndhārī* (right eye). Indra *devatā*.
5. *Hastijihvā* (left eye). Varuṇa *devatā*.
6. *Pūṣā* (right ear). Īśvara *devatā*.
7. *Yaśasvinī* (left ear). Brahmā *devatā*.
8. *Kuhū* (excretory organ). Pṛthvī *devatā*.
9. *Alambuṣā* (reproductive organ). Sūrya *devatā*.
10. *Śaṁkhinī* (navel). Candra *devatā*.

***Śṛṅgārādi rasa* (10)**

1. *Śṛṅgāra.*
2. *Vīra.*
3. *Karuṇa.*
4. *Adbhuta.*
5. *Hāsya.*
6. *Bhayānaka.*
7. *Bībhatsa.*
8. *Raudra.*
9. *Śānta.*
10. *Prema bhakti* or *jñāna rasa.*

Advaitic Concept in 11

***Jñāna-sādhana* (11)**

1. *Viveka* [discrimination between the eternal and non-eternal].
2. *Vairāgya* [dispassion].
3. *Ṣaṭ-sampatti* [sixfold mental disciplines].
4. *Mumukṣutā* [desire for liberation].
5. *Guru upasatti* — approaching a *guru* according to the prescribed rules.
6. *Śravaṇa* [listening to scriptures].
7. *Tattva jñāna abhyāsa* [assimilation of the teaching].
8. *Manana* [removal of doubts].
9. *Nididhyāsana* [removal of habitual notions].
10. *Manonāśa* — here mind refers to the gross aspect with the *guṇas*, *rajas* and *tamas* that has overpowered *sattva*, and destruction means by *brahmābhyāsa* the

rajas and *tamas* are subdued and *sattva guṇa* overpowers.

11. *Vāsanā-kṣaya* [weakening the power of impressions].

Advaitic Concepts in 12

***Anātma-dharma* (12)**

1. *Anitya* [non-eternal].
2. *Vināśī* [destructible].
3. *Aśuddha* [impure due to ignorance].
4. *Nānā* [many].
5. *Kṣetra* [gross].
6. *Āśrita* [supported].
7. *Vikārī* [changing].
8. *Paraprakāśya* [illumined].
9. *Hetumān* [effect].
10. *Vyāpya* — limited (limited by space, time and another entity).
11. *Saṅgī* [related].
12. *Āvṛtta* [concealed].

***Ātma-dharma* (12)**

1. *Nitya* — devoid of origination and destruction.
2. *Avyaya* — free from growth or decay.
3. *Śuddha* — free from impurities like *māyā* and *avidyā*.
4. *Eka* — without homogeneous difference.
5. *Kṣetrajña* — knower of the body.
6. *Āśraya* — substratum.
7. *Avikriyā* — unchanging.
8. *Svaprakāśa* — self-luminous.

9. *Hetu* — is both the intelligent and material cause of the universe, like the spider spinning its web and growth of nail and hair on the body.
10. *Vyāpaka* — unlimited (complete).
11. *Asaṅgī* — free from relations like homogeneous, hetrogeneous and internal.
12. *Anāvṛtta* — devoid of concealment.

***Brāhmaṇa vrata* (12)**

1. *Jñāna* [knowledge of *dharma*].
2. *Satya* [truthfulness].
3. *Śama* [mental discipline].
4. *Dama* [sensory discipline].
5. *Śruta* — study of scriptures.
6. *Amātsarya* — devoid of jealousy or devoid of intolerance on the prosperity of another.
7. *Lajjā* [shy].
8. *Titikṣā* [endurance].
9. *Anasūyā* — free from fault-finding, superimposing defects on virtues.
10. *Yajña* [performance of rituals].
11. *Dāna* [charity].
12. *Dhairya* — control over desire and anger.

***Mahattā hetu dharma* (12)**

1. *Dhanāḍhyatā* [wealth].
2. *Abhijana* — family.
3. *Rūpa* [form].
4. *Tapa* [austerity].
5. *Śruta* — study of scriptures.

6. *Oja* — effulgence of sense-organs.
7. *Teja* [brilliance].
8. *Prabhāva* [dignity].
9. *Bala* [strength].
10. *Pauruṣeya* [humanness].
11. *Buddhi* [intelligence].
12. *Yoga* [discipline].

Advaitic Concept in 13

Bhāgavata *dharma* (13)

Qualities of a devotee.

1. Seeing the contrary to the result of *sakāma karma.*
2. Seeing sorrow and unsteadiness of wealth, house, son, etc.
3. Seeing the perishable nature of result of the other world.
4. Approaching a *guru* for knowledge of *Brahman.*
5. Reverence to *guru* as Almighty and service to *guru.*
6. Total surrender to God.
7. Experience of self with devotion and dispassion. Association with noble ones.
8. Cleanliness, austerity, endurance, silence.
9. Study of one's own scriptures, straightforwardness, non-violence and balanced mind with regard to pairs of opposites (like cold–heat, endurance of extremes).
10. Vision of God in everything.
11. Seclusion (non-binding with house), simple clothes, contentment.
12. Vision of God in everything and in God the vision of everything.

13. Non-identification with birth, action, class, stage of life, etc. and absence of mineness and otherness attitude.

Advaitic Concept in 14

***Tripuṭī* (14)**

Sense-organ adhyātma	*Presiding Deity adhidaiva*	*Sense Object adhibhūta*
Triad of sense-organs of knowledge		
1. Hearing	Dik	Sound
2. Touch	Vāyu	Touch
3. Sight	Sūrya	Form
4. Taste	Varuṇa	Taste
5. Smell	Aśvinikumāras	Smell
Triad of sense-organs of action		
6. Speech	Agni	Speech
7. Hand	Indra	Grasping
8. Feet	Vāmana	Locomotion
9. Reproductive	Prajāpati	Enjoyment
10. Excretory	Yama	Removal of waste
Triad of internal organ		
11. Mind	Candra	Resolution
12. Intellect	Brahmā	Conviction
13. Memory	Vāsudeva	Recollection
14. I-ness	Rudra	I-identity

Advaitic Concept in 15

***Māyā nāma* (15)**

Different names of *māyā*.

1. *Māyā.*
2. *Avidyā.*
3. *Prakṛti.*
4. *Śakti.*
5. *Satyā.*
6. *Mūlā.*
7. *Tūlā.*
8. *Yoni.*
9. *Avyaktā.*
10. *Avyākṛta.*
11. *Ajā.*
12. *Ajñāna.*
13. *Tamas.*
14. *Tucchā.*
15. *Anirvacanīyā.*

Advaitic Concept in 16

Kalā (16)

See *Praśnopaniṣad* 6.4.

1. *Hiraṇyagarbha.*
2. *Śraddhā.*
3. Space.
4. Air.
5. Fire.
6. Water.
7. Earth.
8. Ten sense-organs.
9. Mind.

10. Food.
11. Ability.
12. Austerity.
13. *Mantra.*
14. Rites.
15. Worlds.
16. Name.

Thus ends the sixteenth digit of *Vicāracandrodaya* titled "Concise Lexicon of Vedānta".

śrī vicāracandrodayaṁ śuddhāṁ dhiyaṁ samāpya
vicāryeti parānandaṁ tattvajñānamavāpya.

Thus ends the text *Vicāracandrodaya* (composed for) clarity of thought.

May one take to enquiry and obtain the highest knowledge and absolute peace.

Index of Advaitic Concepts in Kalā 16

Mokṣa dvārapāla (4)

Yama (5)
Yoga bhūmikā (4), (5)

Rasa (6)
Rūpa (7)

Lakṣaṇā (2)
Lakṣaṇa doṣāḥ (3)
Liṅga (6)

Vacanādi (5)
Varṇa (4)
Vartamāna jñāna pratibandha (4)
Vartamāna jñāna pratibandha nivṛtti hetu (4)
Vākya (2)
Vāda (2)
Vādādi (3)
Veda kāṇḍa (3)
Vedāṅga (6)
Vikāra (6)
Vidhi vākya (3)
Viparīta-bhāvanā (2)
Vivekādi (4)
Vyasana (7)

Śabda (2)
Śabda-saṅgati (2)
Śabda-pravṛtti-nimitta (4)
Śabda śakti grahaṇa hetu (8)
Śabdādi (5)
Śamādi (6)
Śarīra (3)
Śāstra (6)
Śravaṇādi (3)
Śravaṇādi phala (3)
Śṛṅgārādi rasa (10)

Sampatti (2)
Sambandha (3)
Saṁśaya (2)
Saṁsāra (9)
Samādhi (2), (6)
Samādhi aṅga (8)
Samādhi vighna (4)
Saṁnyāsa (4)
Suṣupti (3)
Suṣuptyādi (3)
Sūkṣma-śarīram (2)
Sūtra (6)
Sthūla bhūta (5)
Sthūla-śarīram (2)
Sparśa (4)
Svapna (3)

Hetvādi (3)
Hetvābhāsa (5)

Word Index